**Chupi** and **Luke Sweetman** are the teenage children of Irish writer Rosita Sweetman. Aged eighteen and fifteen, they were obliged to relearn what to eat when Chupi was found to have multiple food intolerances. Unwilling to eat a diet of brown rice and stewed soy beans, they found a way to continue eating the things they loved while still being healthy, e.g. The Green Margarita, Caesar Salad with Smoky Chicken, and Homemade French Fries. All organic, of course. They've now set out on a mission to save the world from risky food. They currently live in Wicklow, Ireland. **PATRICIA QUINN** is a nutritionist and kinesiologist who specializes in working with children. Quinn lives in Ireland with her husband Michael and four sons.

THE COMPLETE ALLERGY COOKBOOK

# What to Eat When You Can't Eat Anything

## CHUPI AND LUKE SWEETMAN

Foreword by **PATRICIA QUINN**

Photography by **SUKI STUART**

Food Styling by **CHUPI SWEETMAN AND
SUKI STUART**

Marlowe & Company
New York

WHAT TO EAT WHEN YOU CAN'T EAT ANYTHING: *The Complete Allergy Cookbook*

Copyright © 2004 Chupi and Luke Sweetman
Foreword © 2004 Patricia Quinn
Photographs © 2004 Suki Stuart

Published by
Marlowe & Company
An Imprint of Avalon Publishing Group Incorporated
245 West 17th Street • 11th floor
New York, NY 10011

**AVALON**
publishing group incorporated

Originally published in Ireland by Gill & Macmillan
This edition published by arrangement

Library of Congress Control Number: 2004108705

ISBN 1-56924-411-1

9 8 7 6 5 4 3 2 1

*Designed by Pauline Neuwirth, Neuwirth and Associates, Inc.*

Printed in Canada
Distributed by Publishers Group West

**Luke** and **I** would like to dedicate this to Granny, who couldn't boil an egg, and to Granddad, who taught her how; to Michael and Patricia, our inspirational adopted grandparents; to Brian, our comrade in culinary crime; to Vanilla, the world's funkiest cat; and, of course, to our dearest "Momager."

Cheers!

# Contents

# Foreword

O**N A LOVELY** day in May, the Sweetman family of Chupi, Luke, and Rosita came into my life. Chupi had come with her mom for nutritional counseling and kinesiology. Chupi's history, given by Rosita and herself, included years of unexplained ill health. From questions answered by both Rosita and Chupi, it became very clear that a lot of the functions of our bodies that we healthy types take for granted were not happening for Chupi. Because her food was not being absorbed, her natural defense mechanisms were deprived of minerals and vitamins vital for healthy immunity, and the fats essential for healthy physical, mental, and emotional development. Years of chronic ill health and stress, plus a water supply that was not suitable for drinking or even cooking, had taken a huge toll on Chupi's health. In spite of all this, I found Chupi to be a happy, contented teenager with lots of enthusiasm for living and great ambition.

As is increasingly common among the people who attend my clinic, Chupi's digestion turned out to be a big part of the problem. It was failing to absorb her food and her intestinal immunity was poor, due to a proliferation of yeasts and unfriendly bacteria. The domino effect was poor resistance to infection, poor quality blood, poor healing ability, and multiple food intolerances.

The priority was to put my tried and tested structure in place, to encourage Chupi's body to heal itself:

1. A menu full of good, natural, tasty whole foods.
2. Perfectly clear water to drink, cook, and bathe in.
3. Getting all the defense mechanisms back to work with good food, good water, rest, exercise, and sunshine.
4. Chupi would need to rest for a few minutes before, and again after, each meal.

5. She would take an acidophilus supplement to boost her natural defense mechanisms, boost her digestive ability, and help her to fully absorb her good food.

6. Changing her menu included switching to completely unprocessed food: yeast-free, dairy-free, wheat-free and sugar-free, additive-, color-, and preservative-free.

As with all my patients, it was a real challenge for the family. When they went home there was literally nothing they could eat. Two starving teenagers and a very depleted mom. What a shock! But they fully took on what I had pre-scribed and gradually they learned how to cope as a family.

During Chupi's next visit, a wonderful summer day, it became obvious that she was on the road to recovery. She was extremely hungry, an excellent sign of life, because her body was like a plant adapting to new food. She, her mom, and Luke were all involved in cooking wonderful foods—and they were loving them. We arranged a meeting where we could discuss this new adventure in food, cooking, and creativity.

We agreed to share their new cooking creations with the recipes our family had been collecting for years, many of them adapted from our own mothers' healthy dishes. To make them even healthier, we had moved away from com-mercial wheat, cut out refined sugar, yeasts, and molds, and introduced a wide range of flours, beans, seeds, nuts, and vegetables, all organically produced where possible. As a family, we had been practicing what we preached for the past thirty years. This had proved to be the biggest step toward good health. We did not cut out meat, we just reduced it in favor of lots more vegetables, brown rice, and pastas. When we do eat meat, we try to eat only organically produced, additive-free products.

The road to good health rests in the quality, quantity, preparation, cooking, and, very importantly, the serving of beautiful, unadulterated food. It is life-giving, blood-building, bone-creating, brain-nurturing, mood-healing, emotionally satisfying, and tastes wonderful. This is what Rosita, Chupi, and Luke were dis-covering. They found that their craving for unnatural, unwholesome foods faded away gradually, because whole foods are so satisfying.

Following our discussions, we decided to have a "tasting" day and share our cooking experiences. My husband Michael and I drove to the Sweetman home, the trunk of our car laden with chickpea and chicken casserole with herbs in organic tomato sauce, muffins made of whole meal flour, fruit, and a bottle of apple juice to celebrate! When we brought our contribution to the kitchen, Luke was cooking a wonderful steak with tons of vegetables, Rosita had a made beautiful vegetable soup with homemade stock, and Chupi had made spelt farls and spelt biscuits (Italian, twice-baked biscuits). Chupi and Luke had also made delicious date and orange squares, which emitted an aroma of warm welcome and a warmer taste sensation.

As we exchanged recipes, a thought planted itself: we should gather all the work of both houses together. Everyone was benefiting, our conversations were exhilarating, we were seeing the family's health change. Why not collaborate? We decided to gather up our learning and our recipes, and put them together into an allergy cookbook for all those who found themselves in the same position as Rosita, Chupi, and Luke. The book would be for allergy sufferers, for the very sensitive, the not-so-sensitive, and for those who want to eat beautiful food—perfectly well people who wish to remain in good health. This idea coincided with Chupi and Luke studying for their final exams—at home. A busy time all round!

The change of every season is an acknowledged strain on the body, and all the more so for the very young, teens, and the elderly—the sensitive. Our family meetings to discuss food and health became ideal opportunities to monitor Chupi's health through the seasons of the year. Each season's change meant a change for her: seasonal food, local produce, careful pacing of her energy. If the change of the season is from spring to a glorious May or June, this is a plus factor. Our Irish summers and springs seem to be wetter, damper, and less sunny than before, so as often happens at the end of summer and fall, overnight we can find ourselves in new weather. This is where we need to balance with the environment. Because young people tend to work hard and play hard, this is a difficult lesson to learn—but it pays great dividends in protection from winter chills.

After having been part of an allergic family myself, and taking care of severely allergic families for thirty years, it's clear to me that it is always necessary to find a replacement food for the one removed, however temporarily.

Most people are sensitive to foods they (probably) eat far too regularly. Traditional eating with the seasons in past times was a form of protection against developing sensitivities, but today we are encouraged to eat our favorite foods all year round. Real allergic reactions are infrequent, but they are increasing due to the drastic changes in our eating habits and the ways in which our food is produced using chemicals and pesticides.

Both Chupi and Luke achieved tremendous success in their studies and exams. Chupi decided to take a year off instead of going to college, in order to write this cookbook. With great zest and creativity the recipes were tried, tested, and committed to paper. As we now read through the manuscript just after Christmas 2002, we are excited: the aromas jump off the pages with the wonderful combinations of foods, herbs, and spices. Good health begins with your choice of food. It manifests itself in the dishes prepared in your kitchen as it nourishes the body today and creates the health of tomorrow.

Daily, in my practice, people ask me what to eat and where they can find a book that shows them what to eat: after thirty years of searching, this is that book.

—Patricia Quinn

# The Story
# of Food

*I*N THIS AFFLUENT wedge of the planet, food is not the problem. Here in the West we are surrounded by (literally) mountains of food. Food is everywhere—in supermarkets, restaurants, corner shops, theaters, shopping centers, fast-food outlets, even garages. The problem, however, is what to eat of the food that abounds, how to discriminate so that our food supports and nourishes us as often as possible, makes us smack our lips and yell "Wow! That was delicious." The irony is that the more food there is in our Western world, the more food-related illnesses appear, everything from allergies to obesity to cancer.

Our journey into what to eat began in the spring of 2000. Chupi was lying on the sofa and I was listening to an afternoon radio program on different alternative medicine practices: homoeopathy, aromatherapy, etc. It was a very simple series, with a short introduction by the host, followed by an interview with the chosen practitioner. This week's turn was nutrition. To be honest, nutrition had never been a subject of passionate interest to me, but within minutes of listening to Patricia Quinn's clear-as-a-bell voice, I was riveted.

At the time, Chupi (then sixteen), Luke (then thirteen), and I were in health-hell. Chupi was just barely coping with daily living. Everyone we consulted gave us a different outcome, a different remedy, a different diagnosis. Chupi recoiled from them all, and I, being the mom, was borderline insane with anxiety.

Now here was Patricia Quinn, a clear small voice in the babbling wilderness. She talked about the process of illness: fatigue that doesn't respond to rest; growing irritability; symptoms; and finally, illness. Her "doctors" were sunlight and fresh air, pure water and good food, proper exercise and sufficient rest. Neither illness nor health is random or inexplicable: they occur because of what has happened to us (or what we have done to ourselves). We can (and should) be actively involved in our own healing, following very simple guidelines, starting with rigorously sorting out our nutrition. As Darina Allen once famously remarked, none of us would dream of putting unreliable fuel into our precious cars, yet we routinely put the most unreliable fuel into our bodies. We really are what we eat.

When Patricia saw Chupi for the first time, she diagnosed, along with other problems, an extremely severe Candida albicans infestation. Candida albicans, a yeast common to our digestive systems, usually becomes a problem—sometimes a life-threatening one—when a combination of factors trigger an explosion/overgrowth. The most common trigger is overuse of antibiotics (these wipe out the friendly bacteria in the gut and the ever opportunistic Candida takes hold), and then too much sugar, yeast, and refined, processed wheat in the diet, along with prolonged stress. Candida keeps its hold and gets ever stronger as a weakened immune/digestive system is unable to reassert control by normal methods.

The only cure is to go off all sugar and yeast and any foods that have any traces of yeast or mold. No cookies, no cake, no store-bought pizzas, no fast foods, no alcohol, no vinegar, no store-bought condiments are allowed. As Patricia explained, the only way to control Candida is to stop feeding it. (There is no conventional cure for Candida, in fact conventional medicine's overuse of antibiotics is centrally implicated in the huge rise of Candida in the West. Candida sufferers are forced to take a natural path to healing.) Our task was twofold: to get Chupi off all Candida-feeding foods, and to build her health back up by putting her on a good, clean, healthy diet.

The first few weeks of the diet were pandemonium. Chupi was permanently starving. Luke and I were permanently cooking. No yeast and no sugar meant no supermarket-bought food and no processed or precooked food, since virtually all such food is bulked up with wheat, yeast, sugars, and additives such as monosodium glutamate (MSG). For those of you who pride yourselves on living clean, just think MSG, the most common flavor-enhancing substance around, is apparently the second most addictive substance on the planet, crack cocaine being the first.

Gradually, as Chupi's system got stronger and Luke and I got better in the kitchen, our diet (and stamina) improved. We found friends who ordered whole foods and would put in an extra order for us. The same friends told us of a local organic farm where you can buy boxes of organic, seasonal vegetables every week. A health food shop opened locally. We discovered the Temple Bar Organic Food Market in Dublin and went there every Saturday without fail.

One of the biggest problems we encountered was finding recipes that didn't involve soaking obscure beans for 100 years, cooking them for 500 years, then covering the resultant goo with concentrated apple juice. Chupi and Luke were teenagers, they needed nutritious and tasty food—obscure beans just weren't going to do the trick. We had to stick to the diet, and if we were going to succeed, we had to make it delicious. This cookbook was born, like many good ideas, points out Patricia, at the kitchen table. Chupi was armed with notebook and pen, with Luke and I calling out—turmeric, one teaspoon! Two cloves garlic, crushed! One can organic tomatoes!—as we assembled an evening's concoction.

This is an incredibly exciting time to be interested in food. With many serious diseases, with serious consequences for us humans now endemic in animal and bird populations (salmonella and avian flu in factory-farmed chickens, and mad cow disease in cattle), and cancer rates rising at terrifying rates throughout the Western world, more and more people are beginning to question the policies pursued by the giant food corporations since the middle of the last century. As Marion Nestle, Professor of Nutrition at New York University, points out in her book *Food Politics* (University of California Press), America has been able to feed its entire population twice over for many years now; so the problem for giant food corporations is not how to produce more food but how to get people to eat more of the food that is produced, and how to add value to existing foods. Essentially, in America, behemoths worth billions and billions of dollars, such as Philip Morris, Coca-Cola, and Procter and Gamble, savagely compete in an already saturated market desperately trying to get people to eat more food, that has had more done to it. I'm talking about chemically grown foods with so much added fat, salt, sugar, MSG, and additives, they barely should be classified as foods at all.

As Nestle writes in her conclusion, "We select diets in a marketing environment in which billions of dollars are spent to convince us that nutrition advice is so confusing, and eating healthfully so impossibly difficult, that there is no point in bothering to eat less of one or another food product. . . ." Scary stuff, eh?

Chemicals of course are one of the scariest problems of all in food production. If chemicals and pesticides kill weevils, greenfly, and all those other creepy crawlies that make life difficult for the food producer, then surely they're going to harm us too?

The food may look great on the supermarket shelves, but those glossy bright-red apple skins have been produced by chemicals, not by nature. The buildup of toxins in our bloodstream, kidneys, and livers will inexorably produce illness. In the globalization of food production and marketing, real food has never been so compromised—genetically engineered, drenched in pesticides, stored for far too long. More and more health practitioners see the overproduction of yeast and mold in our systems—as a result of our sugar- and yeast-dependent diet—as the simmering cauldron from which a raft of modern-day illnesses, from thrush to chronic fatigue syndrome, MS, asthma, and cancer, develop. Cooking real, organic, natural, additive-free food has never been more important—for everyone in the family. We believe that eating Green (our name for eating organic), is no longer a lifestyle choice but an absolute necessity.

But, an end to doom and gloom! Here are our recipes for good—and lasting, we hope—health. Where possible, the ingredients are organic; they are also sugar-free, MSG-free, wheat-free (we use spelt flour in all the recipes), yeast- and mold-free, and of course GE-free. They are for anyone suffering from Candida or food intolerances, but they're also—we hope you'll agree—delicious, and really good for everyone in the family, from baby to Granny.

This is our story, the story of the *What to Eat When You Can't Eat Anything* cookbook. Our hope is that all of you, whether suffering from health problems or not, will enjoy every single recipe in our book. As you get more and more into the story of cooking and food, you'll find food time becomes "real time" where all of the household, family or friends, are involved. Meals will become what they truly should be: wonderful thanksgiving feasts, scrumptious and bursting with health, offering all the fruits of Mother Nature.

Enjoy!

—Rosita Sweetman

# The Green Diet

**W**HEN WE REFER to a food as Green, this doesn't mean that it is or should be moldy! Green is what we call our diet and the foods we find acceptable. None of our ingredients will harm you if you are sensitive. You may, however, have a particular problem; if so, you need to know as much about food as possible, so read on.

Diet affects everyone. Young and old, healthy and not so healthy, we are shaped and controlled by what we eat. If there is no energy in our food, should we be surprised when we have no energy? And if we eat food that is so processed it's poisonous, should we be surprised when our bodies show symptoms of poisoning?

When we sensitive types examine our diet, we need to consider the differences between allergies and intolerances. An allergy is systemic; it involves the whole body rejecting and mobilizing to fight a foodstuff, sometimes with very dangerous results, e.g. anaphylactic shock. But a lot of what appear to be food allergies are in fact food intolerances. A food intolerance produces similar symptoms to a food allergy, but the reaction is not as violent because it is not systemic. We are born with an allergy as part of our system. Intolerances are developed for various reasons, such as stress. When the body is stressed, it becomes unable to cope with the most toxic foods.

The reactions in both intolerances and allergies may appear to be very similar, which is why it's hard to tell the difference, but with practice, experience, and a little time and energy we can learn the difference. It is important to be able to tell the difference because, in general, intolerances can in greater part be overcome, but allergies need to be carefully managed.

This section of the book is specifically designed for those of you who would like more information on diets. We list the six main causes of allergies and intolerances: wheat, sugar, yeast, dairy products, gluten, and artificial additives, with a description of each food, symptoms of reactions to each food, why you could be intolerant, how to remove the food from your diet, and what to replace it with. We also give what we hope is some useful information regarding organic foods. In addition, there is a guide on when our recipes should be eaten. The recipes are in three categories: ultrasensitive, sensitive, and unsensitive. This section should help in your search for a better understanding of food and its relationship with your body. When Chupi was diagnosed we remember how confusing and depressing the allergy books we read were, and her new diet centered around beans. So we have tried to make these recipes as intelligible and interesting as possible.

## WHEAT

Grain is a wonderful substance, nourishing and health-giving, but by the time most grains reach us they are nothing more than a worthless plumper. Wheat, often labeled as starch or modified starch, is a perfect example of this. When commercially produced wheat arrives at your table, it will have been covered in pesticides and herbicides, grown on depleted soil with the aid of artificial fertilizers, and the nutritious germ and bran will have been removed. All we are left with is a "powder" that will swiftly become glue when eaten. Even those with the most ironclad digestion will have some problem with commercial wheat, and to those who are sensitive it's a nightmare. (Some people are not wheat intolerant but are intolerant to the junk used on commercial wheat, so bear this in mind.)

**Symptoms of intolerance:** A powdery feeling in the mouth, especially in the morning, irritable bowel syndrome (IBS), bloating, painful digestion, constipation, diarrhea, acid stomach, weight gain (or severe weight loss in celiac disease).

**Replacement:** Wheat is in all—unless specifically labeled wheat-free—baking, breads, buns, pasta, flours, nearly all processed food, instant meals, and takeout food as a bulking agent. When in doubt, read the label. We recommend you remove all "normal" wheat from your diet. Replacing it depends on how intolerant you are; if you have only mild problems with wheat or feel you could do with a boost, then replace it with organic wheat and organic wheat products, using these as normal. If you are sensitive to wheat, replace it with organic spelt flour (available in health food stores). This flour is very similar to wheat, but tastier, and perfect for people with a wheat intolerance. You can use organic spelt products as you would wheat products. If you are highly wheat intolerant, or celiac, then you will need to be very careful. Use rice, maize (corn), and gram flours, millet grain and a small amount of organic oats. Stay on this diet for four weeks then slowly introduce organic spelt flour; if your symptoms return, go back to the exclusion diet until you feel you're ready to try again. It is hard to say how long this can take: some people need only a few weeks, others longer. But in general we have found that 99 percent of people can tolerate, and enjoy, organic spelt.

## SUGAR

Sugar is the enemy. A highly processed "food" of no nutritional value, sugar confuses the body by providing false highs followed by compensatory lows. It encourages yeast overgrowth and is highly addictive. Few people know they are sugar intolerant, yet everyone could do with excluding it from their diet. This is not as easy as it may seem, however, as there are many sources of hidden sugar. Manufacturers realize this, and replace sugar content with artificial sweeteners which are equally bad (see Artificial Additives, page 10). In Eric Shlosser's book, *Fast Food Nation*, he estimates that the average American consumes 52 teaspoons of sugar per day, most of it hidden.

**Symptoms of intolerance:** Mood swings, Candida and other yeast-related problems (e.g. acne, hypoglycemia, skin problems, general itchiness).

**Replacement:** Sugar is found in nearly all processed foods, sweets and treats, and takeout food unless they are specifically labeled sugar-free. Most sugar-free items, however, contain unpleasant sweeteners. Ask for advice from your local health food shop on alternatives to sugar-sweetened soft drinks and other products. Read the section called Yummy Treats (page 135) for help too. If a recipe requires sugar, first consider if it really needs sweetening and, if it does, use local honey, rice syrup, or maple syrup. When you give up sugar, honey will be your savior. Sugar is also widely used in processed, prepacked, ready-made, and takeout meals: I'd recommend you eat none of these unless you are absolutely sure they are sugar-free, and even then . . .

## YEAST

Yeasts and molds are living organisms that thrive in warm, damp conditions, growing at enormous rates. When you eat a slice of bread, in that bread there are thousands of live yeast organisms passing through your stomach, and arriving in your warm, hospitable gut. The yeasts settle in and start to grow. If you are in full health your body's immune system will counteract them. But if your immune system is weak or you have just received a course of antibiotics, then the yeast will continue to grow. One particular yeast, Candida albicans, can turn into a parasite (an organism that lives off another organism—in this case you) breaking through the delicate intestinal lining and allowing undigested food to leak into the bloodstream. Many people are allergic to yeast without knowing it. Patricia and Michael Quinn have written a book called *The Silent Disease* about Candida/yeast overgrowth. In the West we eat a diet and live a life conducive to yeast overgrowth: we eat a lot of sugar, which feeds the yeast. We consume a lot of other yeasts, for example in alcohol, follow a poor, junk-filled diet, and live our lives constantly stressed, allowing our immune systems to remain below par. Yeast overgrowth is also a major factor in intolerances—in fact in some cases it is the cause. If you remove all yeasts from your diet, you will see huge improvements.

**Symptoms of intolerance:** Candida and related problems, acne, eczema, dandruff, psoriasis, fungal infections, irritable bowel syndrome, diarrhea, constipation, thrush, allergies.

**Replacement:** Unfortunately yeasts are found in all breads (except soda bread), alcohol, mushrooms, vinegars, soy sauces, and tofu. You may be panicking at the thought of excluding all these products from your diet, but they can be replaced. For the breads use soda bread—if you can eat wheat and dairy products there are a few nice store-bought ones; if not, make you own using our recipe (page 152), Sourdough breads are delicious as long as you buy good ones. There is no alcohol replacement, you just have to give it all (yes, all) up. If you are absolutely desperate you can try very pure alcohol such as vodka—low in yeast. This won't work for everybody, however, and I wouldn't recommend it. Some people can eat mushrooms, others cannot. They should be avoided for the first few weeks at least. Vinegar can be replaced with freshly squeezed lemon juice. For soy sauce, just leave it out, it's only a trendy flavor enhancer. You can try it again when you feel up to it. Tofu is best avoided during the initial stages of your new diet, but it can be reintroduced later.

## DAIRY PRODUCTS

This means all milk and milk products, but for our book we have primarily excluded cow's milk, as most people who are intolerant to cow's milk can take goat's and sheep's milk produce. We don't use much dairy in our recipes anyway, so don't worry if you can't have it. Dairy intolerance is one of the most prevalent and the only answer is to reduce the amount of dairy you eat. Carefully managed and used sparingly, such products can be a tasty addition to our diets.

**Symptoms of intolerance:** Acne, eczema, coated tongue, diarrhea, blocked or runny nose, sinusitis, catarrh, Candida, thrush.

**Replacement:** Milk, cream, milk solids, half-fat solids, and whey are all dairy. Dairy clearly means all butter, cheese, milk, yogurt, creams, and ice creams. It also tends to be in processed foods, such as ready-made soups. There are two paths to change: you can remove all dairy produce from your diet, especially if you are dairy intolerant, and replace with our list below; or you can remove all nonorganic and hidden dairy products but use very small amounts of organic dairy. We now follow the second path, having tried the first for a year.

You will see that a few of our recipes use organic bio-live natural yogurt, which I could eat even when I was intolerant, as it's wonderfully soothing and packed with good bacteria, a great help if you're yeast-intolerant.

Replace butter with a good extra-virgin olive oil or organic butter; cheese can be replaced with organic goat's or sheep's cheese. Many people can tolerate goat or sheep products, even if they can't have cow's milk cheese. Replace cow's milk with oat, soy, rice, or goat's milk. Yogurt can be replaced with organic bio-live natural yogurt, which also works as a cream substitute. If you can't have that, try a soy cream. Be careful, as some brands have lots of other harmful ingredients in them. Instead of ice cream, use soy ice cream or discover the joy of sorbet. Try Mango Sorbet (page 141).

## ARTIFICIAL ADDITIVES

So much of the food we now eat contains additives—a packet of chips that doesn't contain E621 is a rarity. And yet as consumers, we know very little about these additives. Take E621, also known as monosodium glutamate (MSG). Used as a flavor enhancer in chips and nearly every prepackaged food, MSG is a boon to food companies: add a dollop and everyone, young and old, will want to eat your product. Yet MSG is dangerous to babies and children, bad for asthma and hyperactivity, and is highly addictive. Why would MSG affect you if you have a specific allergy? Well, if you have an allergy, your body is not at its full strength, so it is very important to be careful that everything you eat will strengthen your body as well as stimulate your taste buds. This also applies to artificial sweeteners. Many people, for example diabetics, give up sugar, rightly believing it to be bad for them. They then replace sugar with sweeteners, but artificial sweeteners are as bad as sugar—they are an empty food. One of the first mistakes I made when I gave up sugar was to eat a packet of sugar-free candy that contained lots of artificial sweeteners. The effects were as bad, if not worse, than my reaction to normal sugar. So remember, if you don't know what it is, don't eat it.

**Symptoms of intolerance:** Sudden onset of heartburn, skin reactions, itchiness, dizziness, stomach upset, mouth ulcers, asthma attack.

**Replacement:** First identify what products you buy that contain potentially questionable ingredients. This will include nearly all processed, packaged, ready-made meals and all candies and treats. Eliminate them from your diet. However, good chips can be a savior when you give up everything else, so find a brand you can eat, buy one bag and one apple and enjoy. In general, the plainer the chips the better (e.g. just salt). Try the supermarkets, as there you get a wide selection and can also find the best. Tortilla chips are worth checking out, as there are some very tasty flavors (I had chili and cocoa!) that don't contain any junk. This advice applies to all foods that contain artificial additives—90 percent of the time you will be able to find a food to replace the junk one, the other 10 percent was probably extremely bad for you and best not eaten anyway.

## GLUTEN

Before reading this section, we strongly recommend that you read our wheat section first. The two reactions are so similar that it would be most unfortunate to mistake a gluten allergy/intolerance for the far less complicated wheat allergy/intolerance. Allergic reactions to gluten are becoming more common, and celiac is another name for the true allergic reaction to gluten. Gluten is the "gluey" protein contained in the starchy part of some grains. You can see it at work when you make porridge with oats—the way it sticks together and becomes gluelike is the gluten. If you are allergic to gluten, when you eat any grain containing it, your body will go through the normal digestive process until the gluten reaches the small intestine. Our small intestine is like a long pipe, the inside of which is lined with little digestive "feelers" called villi; these absorb the nutrients from our food. However, if you are allergic to gluten, when it comes into contact with the villi, they swell up and your body simply cannot absorb any nutrients. You also experience a range of unpleasant symptoms.

**Symptoms of intolerance:** Acid stomach, coated tongue, severe weight gain or loss, bloating.

**Replacement:** Gluten is in many grains. All wheat products, including couscous, rye, and oats have a low gluten content, so should be avoided by the true celiac. Barley also has a low gluten content. Spelt flour contains gluten but seems to be tolerated by some—and I stress "some"—people. Considering this, you're going to have to work hard to not eat gluten. No prepackaged/ready-made/bought foods are permitted unless they are from a whole-food supplier who understands the whole issue. You can eat buckwheat, chickpea/gram, cornmeal/maize, millet, and rice products, as they are all gluten-free.

The three main areas where a gluten allergy/intolerance will affect your life are, first, bread; I can't enthuse about gluten-free bread, because it isn't great, but persevere and you'll get through. We do have a good gluten-free tortilla, and a gluten-free bread. Then there's pasta: the two best we've found are rice-and-millet, and buckwheat; the others just seem to dissolve into a goo. Be careful when cooking gluten-free pasta, as it takes much less time to cook than ordinary pasta. Finally, there are candies and treats; we have lots of yummy gluten-free treats, so hopefully they will help.

Try an exclusion diet for three weeks before you commit yourself to a gluten-free life. And, remember, it is possible to overcome a gluten problem. Good luck!

## ORGANIC

Organic farming is a return to traditional farming; no artificial fertilizers, pesticides, or chemicals are used, plants are grown naturally and animals are reared with respect. And with the vast range of genetically engineered foods available on the market today, going organic has never been so important.

**Finding organic products:** Try to locate an organic farm in your area and see if they'll sell you fresh, organic, seasonal vegetables. If you try these, you will notice a difference in taste. Because organic food is far more labor intensive, it costs more, so switching completely to organic may not be feasible all in one shot. Just change the really important foods such as meat. All meat you eat should be organic—there is no need to detail the endless list of problems with "normal" meat (think mad cow disease). You should not expose yourself, or the animals, to these risks. Organic meat can be found in most supermarkets, and your local butcher or farmers' market; if you can't find any, then just ask.

The second most important area in which to go organic is dairy produce. If you're dairy intolerant, then this is irrelevant, but some people who are dairy intolerant can tolerate organic dairy. Try supermarkets for organic dairy—surprisingly enough they tend to be the best source of organic yogurt, butter, cheese, and milk.

As for fruit and vegetables, eat seasonally as much as possible, because food in season tends to be less chemical-laden. As I said above, there will also probably be an organic farm in your area that runs a box scheme. It's often cheaper than the supermarkets, you're supporting your local economy, and you know exactly who is growing your food. The food actually looks and tastes organic, unlike the supermarket stuff! But if all you can get is supermarket organic produce, it's better than nothing.

Then there are grains and pulses, pantry staples. Most are grown with extraordinary amounts of artificial chemicals, so check out the organic alternative in your local health food shop. They will normally supply everything you need and will be happy to help.

# The Kitchen

**W**HEN YOU BEGIN the change to Green eating you will need to review both the food you have in your home and the food you buy. You may, as we have done, change your whole outlook on food and eating, or you will perhaps just want to incorporate some new things into your diet. Either way, your pantry is where to start.

First, look through your cupboards and fridge. Examine the food you eat, read the labels, and prepare to be shocked, bemused, and annoyed. Now chuck out any suspicious foods and replace them with proper food. The most important thing when out shopping is to read the labels on everything. We know that a lot of people are pressed for time, but you need do it only once: look through the foods you have at home, examining the labels of the things you consider as staples. No doubt at least one of them will take you by surprise— do you know what E621 is? And why it's necessary in your Italian–style "health conscious" pizza? Then every time you shop, read the labels of things that you buy occasionally.

Another important thing we have learned in our food forays is that when you have to give something up, you should replace it. We no longer use non-organic wheat flour, or any products containing nonorganic wheat flour, yet we still have breads, biscuits, and pizzas, because we found a replacement flour. Spelt flour is an ancient version of wheat that seems to be digestively perfectly acceptable for people who are wheat intolerant. It even tastes better.

WHAT TO EAT WHEN YOU CAN'T EAT ANYTHING

# The Golden Rules

THESE ARE THE most important qualities a food can possess:

**Organic.** This is no longer a fad—organic farming is here to stay. It heralds a return to traditional farming methods, which are cruelty-, artificial-, chemical-, and, increasingly importantly, GE-free.

**Locally produced.** Such products will be in harmony with your body. Unforced food is healthier and you are also supporting your local community.

**In season.** Out of season means tons of chemicals are used to produce. If you eat seasonally, you get that great "Ooh! It's zucchini" (or other foodstuff)-feeling!

**Minimal amount of processing.** Processing reduces the nutritional content of foods and such food is usually full of junk.

**Brand spankingly fresh.** Fresh food has a higher nutritional content, and of course food just tastes so much better when it's fresh.

**Junk-free.** This may seem obvious, but when you're out shopping, you can sometimes to forget to check if a food is acceptable.

# The Pantry

## OUT

All commercial, nonorganic wheat flours

All yeast

All sugary cereals

All nonorganic wheat pasta and noodles

All artificial flavorings and table salt

All refined sugar and artificial sweeteners

All junk snacks, e.g. commercial chips

Vegetable and nondescript cooking oil

Stock cubes and other flavor enhancers

All ready-made sauces and condiments

All refined rice

Instant coffees and teas

All instant foodstuffs and ready-made meals

## IN

Organic spelt or organic wheat flours, both whole grain and white

Baking soda and wheat-free baking powder

Homemade muesli and granola, junk-free cereals

Organic spelt, wheat, or buckwheat pasta, rice noodles, and millet

A grinder of black pepper and of sea salt

Local organic honey

Organic chips, candies, dates, almonds, popcorn, peanuts

Extra-virgin olive oil and sunflower oil (organic)

A pot of fresh stock and yeast-free bouillon powder

Homemade pesto, Harissa (relish), and salsa

Organic short-grain brown rice and white basmati

Dandelion coffee and herbal teas, e.g. chamomile

Fine ingredients to prepare your own meals: Organic canned tomatoes, chickpeas, kidney beans, mixed beans, tuna, red and green lentils, oats

# The Fridge

## OUT

All processed cheeses

Nonorganic dairy butter and "normal" margarine

All nonorganic dairy milks, including low fat

All artificially flavored yogurts

All non–free-range eggs

All processed suspect sauces and relishes, e.g. mayonnaise, ketchup, and soy sauce

All sugary drinks

All junk convenience foodstuffs

All nonorganic meat

## IN

A selection of organic cheeses, including cheddar and feta

Organic butter

A selection of alternative milks: organic cow's, sheep's, rice, oat, or soy

Organic dairy, bio-live natural and naturally flavored yogurts

Organic, if possible, free-range eggs

Ingredients for mayonnaise, salsa, Harissa (relish), and dressing

Fresh fruit juices, sugar-free fizzy drinks and smoothies

Fresh ingredients

Organic meat: minced beef, chicken fillets, bacon

Organic fruit and veggies: onions, garlic, tomatoes, scallions, potatoes, avocado and seasonal green veggies, like zucchinis in late summer, cabbage in winter, bananas, lemons, and apples

Everything you buy will not meet these criteria all the time, but this is what we should all aspire to. Don't feel overwhelmed if it seems impossible—everyone starts somewhere, and hopefully you'll become so passionate about food and eating, you'll want to find the best. Good luck!

# The Garden

THIS SECTION IS dedicated to Michael "Mr. Green Fingers" Quinn. Why the garden? If you try to buy fresh herbs in a supermarket, you will be met by rows of tiny plastic boxes containing three sprigs of rosemary or six leaves of basil at an exorbitant price. Look at your garden, or your windowsill—surely there's a spot somewhere for a rosemary bush, a few pots of basil, or some chives? Go to your local garden center and buy one rosemary plant—pop it into your garden or into a pretty pot on your windowsill, and watch it thrive. Use sprigs of rosemary when you cook, it is so easy, so cheap, and so delicious. Now that you are hooked, read our list of "must-have" herbs and go get them.

**Basil:** Wonderful in all dishes that contain tomatoes or anything Mediterranean, basil regulates the adrenal system, helping our bodies to relax and cope with stress. Basil grows only in the summer, must be grown in pots, and needs to be watched, as greenfly love it. That said, it is so gorgeous you can forgive these minor faults.

**Bay:** A truly magnificent herb, or should that be tree—we have a bay bush that is now twelve feet high! Don't let that put you off, though. Bay leaves are an essential ingredient in stock and for all roasting dishes.

**Chives:** Chives are perfect when you want the onion hit without the work. They are antibacterial and share other health-giving characteristics with the other members of their family—onions, scallions, and garlic. Very easy to grow, chives take up a minimum of space and produce pretty purple flowers too.

**Mint:** Excellent for enlivening salad dishes, mint cleanses the system wonderfully if you're feeling "heavy." Simple to grow, mint will happily occupy an entire bed to itself. You can contain it by planting it in a large colander.

**Parsley:** Another cleanser, parsley is also very high in vitamin C, perfect if you have the flu. Parsley is an "easy" herb, not so strong as to put people off, so it can be safely added to nearly all dishes as a natural flavor enhancer. Again, it is easy enough to grow, but best grown in pots.

**Rosemary:** Without a doubt my favorite herb. Rosemary and basil have a natural affinity and are gorgeous together. Rosemary works in traditional (potato cakes), Mediterranean (Cianfotta), and our food (fried rice). It is also easy to grow, provided you find a nice dry, free-draining spot.

**Sage:** A robust flavor, sage is best used where you can really taste it, such as in Feta and Sage Relish (page 167), or else as part of a bouquet of herbs in a stew or stock. Sage is a wonderful healer, perfect with lots of honey for sore throats, the flu, or colds. Sage likes the same growing conditions as rosemary, a dry, hot undisturbed spot.

**Thyme:** Where would any stew be without thyme? Thyme is perfect with rosemary and sage, popped in beside any dish to be roasted. Its warm flavor is wonderfully comforting. Like sage, thyme is a great healer, though it is better suited to the lungs. Thyme will happily grow beside sage and rosemary.

# Food Resources

*R*ESOURCES FOR GOOD food are crucial. When you change your eating habits, you also need to change where you shop and what you buy. In "The Kitchen" we dealt with what you buy, here we'll try to help you with where to shop. Remember, though, always to read the label—only you know what you can and can't eat. Don't be fooled if something says "healthy," and just because a package says sugar/dairy/wheat/yeast-free, it doesn't mean it's not packed with other artificial garbage. As Dr. Jane Plant, the British scientist and author of *Your Life in Your Hands*, says, never go out without your glasses and read all labels.

## LOCAL STORES

By local stores we mean the corner market, the butcher, and the deli, each a valuable resource. Mostly ignored in favor of giant supermarkets, local shops are a great ally. Their produce is often less likely to be processed than supermarkets' and they know where the food they stock comes from. Small shops, unlike the supermarkets, don't have the resources to buy food from halfway across the globe and freeze it for months on end, so use this to your advantage. Local food stores tend to be very knowledgeable about their food, so ask what's best and what's organic and local. Create a demand!

## HEALTH FOOD STORES

If you've never been into your local health food store, start today. It may appear intimidating, but persevere and you'll find most staff in these stores are ready and willing to help. They are also good for information on local organic farms that will sell you fresh vegetables, for example, and they're always happy to source anything you need. In these stores, you'll find all pantry staples, e.g. spelt flour, local organic food, and Green packet foods, e.g. falafel mix.

## FARMERS' MARKETS

These are the fastest growing new food outlets at the moment. Farmers' markets are a gift to the Green eater: tasty, organic, just-harvested-this-morning, not-too-expensive food straight from the producer. Could you ask for anything better? Look around your locality, there's bound to be some sort of market near you. At the more upscale markets you'll find tasty treats, e.g. good olive oil, and other specialities. Farmers' markets will supply you with local veggies, fruit, bread, and meat.

Country markets are where you will find free-range eggs, local honey, soda breads, seasonal fruit, and veggies.

## SUPERMARKETS

You may be surprised by what you can now find in your supermarket. Most stock a good range of Green foods and are bowing to the inevitable Green food revolution! They are good for cheap organic pantry staples, like canned tomatoes and organic dairy products.

# Tools of the Trade

**T**O COOK IN both style and comfort, these are the items you will need.

## KNIVES

- Two or three good chef's knives (We use Sabatier). One medium blade (4–5 inches), and one small blade (3 inches) for peeling and paring. Invest in the best you can, as you'll be using them all the time.
- One good bread knife (8–9 inches). Get one with really good teeth and a strong, comfortable handle.

## CHOPPING BOARDS

- Two or three good solid wooden boards for chopping and preparing.

## GADGETS AND GIZMOS

- Knife sharpener: We use the flat kind that sits on the table.
- Garlic press: Try and get the metal kind—the plastic ones tend to snap under pressure.
- Can opener: You need a good strong one.

- Peeler: The metal-blade kind with a bound wooden handle; the plastic ones break and all metal ones hurt your hands.
- Kitchen scissors: A good strong scissors that is kept just for use in the kitchen.
- Box grater: A wonderful gizmo, essential for grating and zesting jobs.
- Potato masher: The all-metal kind is good.
- Pepper mill: Totally essential. Salt mills are good too, but not essential.
- Citrus juice squeezer: Rigid plastic will do, but you can sometimes find beautiful old glass ones.
- Measuring jug: We have a big and a small one. Make sure they have imperial measures. Glass or Pyrex is best.
- Food Scale.
- Whisk: We have one large and one medium.
- Sieve: The old-fashioned metal kind is best.
- Rolling pins: We have two wooden ones, large and small.

## SPOONS

- Two or three wooden spoons and two wooden spatulas. Absolutely essential, we have lots of wooden spoons.
- Metal ladle (for soups, stews, etc.).
- Fish slice.

## POTS AND PANS

- One large heavy-bottomed cast iron frying/sauté pan
- Two medium-size nonstick frying/sauté pans
- Two or three good quality stainless steel pans (large/medium/small)
- Two or three cast iron enameled pans. Le Creuset is best, if expensive, but once you have one you'll have it for life.
- One large roasting pan. The deep enameled pans are best.
- One springform cake pan (6–7 inches).
- One tart pan (11 inches).
- One wire rack for cooling and for cooking.

# ELECTRICAL GEAR

- One handheld electric mixer: This is all you need. You can dispose of your enormous food processor. Once you've got the hang of the hand-held mixer, you'll never take that other complicated, breakable, diffi-cult-to-wash gadget out of the cupboard ever again.

# The Right Recipes for the Right Time

**A**S I'VE SAID before, we believe that when you're intolerant to foods it's not necessarily just a specific food that is a problem, but that your whole body is too stressed and thus unable to cope with certain very intense foods. This was certainly true in our case; we devised the Green diet, through accident, luck, and pure hunger, to enable us to cope with eating. Yet the diet has been so successful that while at the start we needed to be very careful as we were ultrasensitive, the good food has enabled us to progress to foods that we would never have been able to eat while ultrasensitive. We then progressed to a sensitive stage, right up to now where we eat a good, practically unsensitive diet. With this in mind we've divided the recipes into three categories: ultrasensitive, sensitive, and unsensitive. That's not to say the categories aren't interchangeable—these are simply a few guidelines to get you started. Listen to your body and always listen to what it's trying to say to you.

And, oh yeah, relax, you *will* get well.

# Recipes for when you are Ultrasensitive

**ULTRASENSITIVE IS** when you are intolerant to, or not eating, dairy, wheat, sugar, yeast, eggs, and meat. You may be hypoglycemic, with severe Candida, chronic fatigue, or irritable bowel syndrome. Many people who are ultrasensitive tend to be celiac as well. With that in mind, we use all simple foods and cut out all junk (read the Different Diets section for more information on this).

# Recipes for when you are Sensitive

**W**HEN YOU ARE just sensitive, things are improving. Your intolerances will have calmed and you will be feeling better due to abstention from the causes of your problems. Your body will also be picking up, thanks to all the wonderful nutrition it has been getting. So now you can include some more foods in your diet, plus everything in the ultrasensitive section.

You could try one of the pasta dishes now:

# Recipes for when you are Unsensitive

**Y**OU WILL NOW know what your allergies are and what your intolerances were, thus you can decide what is good for you and occasionally eat foods that are strong, like organic dairy. You can eat everything under the previous two headings as well as everything below. Enjoy.

# The Basics

THESE DAYS PEOPLE cook far less than they used to, which means that fewer people actually know how to cook. So here are the basics for the newly converted, and old hands, to cooking.

Cooking is both easy and enjoyable, not a chore to be dreaded. When we cook at home, we all cook—everyone, friends and family. Getting everyone involved when you cook makes it less work and more fun. The more people are involved in the cooking, the greater their interest in food. On this principle, put everyone on the same diet. Even if just one person in a house is sick, it really helps if everyone eats—at least some of the time—as the sensitive person does. Although many people feel they don't have the time to cook, a tasty pasta or soup can be whipped together in the time it takes to prepare convenience foods—and the difference in taste is incredible. Remember, food and cooking should be a joy, not a penance.

Always use the best ingredients, brand spankingly fresh and organic where possible. Organic is not simply about saving the planet, nor is it just about health. It's also about flavor: good ingredients make good food, and you can't get any better than organic. In our recipes we recommend certain foods and ingredients, none of which should be too hard to find. Check out Food Resources if you're having problems (page 20).

Get to know your equipment. We cook on an ancient gas stove, proof that there's no need for appliances. What you do need, however, is to know your equipment. Throughout the recipes we indicate, for example, "a medium heat" or a "low heat"; you will get to know how "low" or "high" suits your stove and what its happy temperatures are. If you're in doubt, always err on the side of caution. For notes on equipment, see Tools of the Trade (page 22).

This is an allergy cookbook, but it is also a food cookbook. In the recipes, we use no sugar or yeast, as we feel they are too problematic. Occasionally we do use organic dairy, based on our personal experience that after an initial exclusion period, a small amount of organic dairy is acceptable and enhances the flavor. For flours we have given the option to use organic wheat, if you want to, in place of spelt flour, but we always use spelt as it's so good. In fact everything is up to you: if something isn't OK, replace it; if something is OK, use it.

—Chupi Sweetman

# Morning Foods

As we know only too well, morning is the most important time to eat, although it is also the most difficult time to eat. One of the things you will find when you switch to Green eating is that you'll be extremely hungry: eating in the morning is vital if you don't want to be gnawing the table leg by 10 A.M.! So our first recipe chapter is called Morning Foods to highlight the importance of morning eating—the opposite of grabbing a cappuccino and croissant on your way to stressville.

In this chapter we hope to show that it is possible to make lots of delicious, hot organic food in a short amount of time, just before you charge out to face the world.

# Pinhead Porridge

*P*ORRIDGE isn't very exciting, nor is it very tasty if the only kind you've tried is the gooey mush made from normal oats. We've found that if you use pinhead oats the change in flavor is incredible. You get a sweet, chewy porridge, delicious with a milk of your choice (oat, rice, soy, goat's, or cow's) and a big dollop of honey. The only downside is you have to soak the oats the night before, but then they only take a few minutes to cook in the morning.

**2 cups pinhead oat flakes**
**6 cups water**
**milk (oat, rice, soy, goat's, or organic cow's)**
**local organic honey**

- Put the oats in a saucepan.
- Cover with 2 inches water. Leave to soak overnight.
- In the morning, put the saucepan on medium heat with another cup of water, and cook for 15–18 minutes, stirring occasionally. The oats are cooked when they've lost their crunch.
- Serve with milk and some honey.

**MAKES 4 SERVINGS**

# Muesli

*M*UESLI, with its mixture of oats, fruits, and nuts, is one of the best ways to start the day. Once you start making your own, you'll never want to look at one of those store-bought, sugar-laden travesties again. And, of course, be creative—add more of what you like and less of what you don't, using our recipe as a template. Another good idea is to make double or triple quantities and store in an airtight jar for during the week when you need an instant boost.

2 cups oat flakes
2 cups jumbo oat flakes
1 cup rye flakes
1 tablespoon dried apricots, washed and quartered
1 tablespoon dried papaya, washed and chopped
1 tablespoon currants, washed
1 tablespoon dates, roughly quartered
1 tablespoon sunflower seeds
1 tablespoon pumpkin seeds
1 tablespoon banana chips
1 tablespoon almonds, chopped

- Put all the ingredients in a large bowl. Mix together and store in an airtight jar.
- Serve with goat's, organic cow's, rice, or soy milk, perhaps topped with a chopped banana or apple and a drizzle of honey.

**MAKES 4 SERVINGS**

**WHAT TO EAT WHEN YOU CAN'T EAT ANYTHING**

# Crunchy Nut Granola

*A*N excellent standby for when the munchies hit! Granola is a good way to start the day. Our blood sugar levels are very low in the mornings and the dried fruit in this recipe raises blood sugar and the grains help to sustain it. Some people prefer granola without the dried fruit—try it both ways to see which you prefer. Granola is also excellent as a dessert, with some bio-live yogurt and fruit. Cooking granola is simple, you just need to keep an eye on it in the oven and take it out when it's golden.

3 tablespoons local organic honey
3 tablespoons sunflower oil
2 cups oat flakes
2 cups jumbo oat flakes
1 tablespoon pumpkin seeds
1 tablespoon almonds, chopped
1 tablespoon Brazil nuts, chopped
1 tablespoon currants, washed
1 tablespoon dates, washed and roughly quartered
½ tablespoon dried papaya, chopped and washed

- Preheat the oven to 275°F.
- Melt the honey and oil in a large saucepan on gentle heat, being careful not to let the mixture come to a boil. When the honey has melted, remove the mixture from the heat.
- Add the remaining ingredients, minus the dried fruit. Stir and mix until well coated. Spread out on a large baking tray and pop into the oven for 30 minutes.
- Halfway through the cooking, remove from the oven and mix thoroughly. Return to the oven. The granola is cooked when it is crisp and golden. Take out of the oven, stir to break up the lumps, and allow to cool. Add the dried fruit and mix again. Store in an airtight container.
- Serve with your favorite milk as a breakfast or snack, or with some stewed fruit as a dessert.

**MAKES 5 SERVINGS**

# Boiled Egg with Toast

*I*F you can tolerate eggs, this is an ideal way to start the day, full of power vitamins and minerals. And who can resist a boiled egg with slices of toasted bread, the ridiculous and the sublime? Try our variation, Coddled Egg, which is perfect comfort food for any age group.

2 cups water
2 free-range eggs
4 slices Soda Bread (page 152)
2 teaspoons organic butter

- Start by boiling 2 cups of water in a small saucepan. When bubbles appear, reduce the heat to a gentle simmer.
- Gently lower the first egg into the water on a tablespoon and do likewise with the second egg. Put the lid on and leave to cook for 3–4 minutes.
- Just before the eggs are ready, toast the Soda Bread until it's brown. Spread all four slices evenly with the butter and cut into thinnish strips.
- Gently take the eggs out of the pot and put into funky eggcups (we use shot glasses!). Serve at once with the toast.

**MAKES 2 SERVINGS**

## Coddled Egg

For Coddled Egg, use the same ingredients as for Boiled Egg with Toast. Proceed as above, but chop the toast into squares. When the eggs are cooked, scoop the insides of both eggs out into 2 pretty cups, chop the mixture up a bit, add the toast squares, mix gently, and season with a pinch of salt and a few twists of pepper.

# Mexican Scrambled Eggs

*A*S well as a wonderful breakfast, scrambled egg makes a good snack. Not many people seem to be able to cook tasty scrambled egg, though—it usually turns out like some kind of yellow rubber! Really it's very simple: just keep your nerve, and don't overcook it. When you think it's nearly done, take the saucepan off the heat, the warmth of the saucepan will finish off the cooking. Anyway, I've never eaten undercooked scrambled egg, have you?

1 large very ripe tomato, chopped into chunks
1 scallion, chopped
organic butter
1 splash extra-virgin olive oil
sea salt and freshly ground black pepper
4 slices Soda Bread (page 152)
2–3 free-range eggs

- In a heavy-bottomed saucepan, sauté the tomato and scallion in the butter and olive oil. Season generously with salt and pepper, Cook on medium heat for 4–5 minutes until the tomato is softish. Remove from the heat and allow to cool while you pop your bread into the toaster.
- Now add the eggs to the tomato and scallion mixture, mixing well so that the yolk and white combine. Put the saucepan back on the heat and cook slowly for 2 minutes, stirring so the egg doesn't stick to the sides of the saucepan or turn to rubber. A moment before the egg is cooked to your taste, take it off the heat—the warmth of the saucepan will finish the cooking.
- Serve immediately with your toast.

**MAKES 2 SERVINGS**

# Fried Tomatoes with Crispy Toast

THIS is a warm, tasty breakfast at any time of the year—although we shouldn't eat too many tomatoes out of season, it's hard to resist. On the weekend when you have the time, try these tomatoes with Mexican Scrambled Eggs (page 39), Sautéed Potatoes with Chives (page 44), and a slice of fried bacon. Absolute indulgence.

1 tablespoon extra-virgin olive oil
3 very ripe tomatoes, sliced about ¼-inch thick
sea salt and freshly ground black pepper
4 slices bread of your choice, for toast (see Excellent Breads pages 151–163)

- Warm the olive oil in a small frying pan. Add the tomatoes and season with a pinch of salt and lots of pepper. Cook on medium heat—not too hot, as you don't want all the tomato juices evaporating.
- Cook for about 5 minutes, until the tomato is soft on both sides. Meanwhile, toast the bread until nice and crispy.

**MAKES 2 SERVINGS**

# Fried Bread

OH rapture, oh joy, oh damn this stuff is so very, very good. Perhaps not the very healthiest of dishes, but you will definitely enjoy it!

**2 tablespoons organic butter**
**2 slices bread of your choice**
**1 tablespoon extra-virgin olive oil**

- Put a pan over medium heat and melt the butter. Add the bread to it. Make sure that you cover both sides of the bread evenly with the melted butter.
- Cook for 2 minutes, 1 minute each side, then add the olive oil and cook for another 2 minutes, or until brown.
- Eat with A New Traditional Breakfast (page 42) or with Fried Tomatoes with Crispy Toast (page 40).

**MAKES 4 SERVINGS**

# A New Traditional Breakfast

THIS is a very strong recipe, so don't eat it when you are weak. Greasy foods are certainly bad, but this breakfast is sautéed in extra-virgin olive oil and, provided you don't eat it for every meal, it's wonderful.

4 tablespoons extra-virgin olive oil
3 large boiled potatoes, sliced ½-inch thick
3 scallions, chopped
sea salt and freshly ground black pepper
4 slices bacon
3 very ripe tomatoes, sliced about ½-inch thick
4 free-range eggs
4 slices bread of your choice

- Coat the bottom of a large pan in the olive oil and heat it over a medium flame. Arrange the potatoes in a single layer on the pan, then sprinkle with the chopped scallions. Season with a pinch of salt and lots of black pepper.
- Now get a second smaller pan, coat it in olive oil, and spread the bacon out on the pan. Season the bacon with a few twists of pepper. Leave both pans to cook for 5 minutes.
- Add the tomatoes to the bacon pan—the oil the bacon is cooking in will make the tomato taste all the better. Turn the potatoes occasionally. Cook the bacon for a few more minutes or until brown. Then take the bacon off the pan on a plate and keep warm.
- Now gently squash the tomatoes (still in the pan) and season with salt and pepper. Leave the tomatoes for 3 more minutes, then take them off the pan and put them on the plate with the bacon.
- Take the potatoes off the pan and put them on the serving plate. Crack the eggs into the pan and fry to your taste. Take the eggs off the pan and put them on separate plates.
- Toast the bread till brown and serve immediately.

**MAKES 4 SERVINGS**

# Banana Smoothies

SMOOTHIES could be considered the Green alternative to milk shakes, but I think that would be overestimating milk shakes and underestimating smoothies. Smoothies are a fresh, sweet, creamy (without cream) drink, suitable for a summer treat, a morning pick-me-up, or when sugar cravings bite. Although we think that if you are having smoothies for breakfast, it's best to use only bananas, you can use other fruit instead. Try mango, strawberries, or any other soft fruit. Early in the morning, however, simplicity is always best.

¾ cup fresh banana, mango, or strawberries, prepared for eating
¾ cup bio-live yogurt or rice, oat, or cow's milk
organic local honey, if desired
ice cubes

- Put the fruit into a blender, add the yogurt or milk, and honey if using, and mix.
- When completely smooth, pour into a tall glass with a few ice cubes. Serve and enjoy.

**MAKES 1 SERVING**

## Yogurt, Honey, and Vanilla Smoothies

If you are dairy intolerant, it's best to avoid these smoothies until your intolerance has leveled out a bit. That said, Chupi has always been dairy intolerant but has never had a problem with organic bio-live natural yogurt. Just try a little bit and see.

½ cup apple juice, freshly pressed
½ cup organic bio-live natural yogurt
2 teaspoons local organic honey
½ teaspoon vanilla extract

- Mix all the ingredients in a blender.
- Serve in a pretty glass.

**MAKES 1 SERVING**

# Sautéed Potatoes with Chives

*P*OTATOES are the most wonderful food—fortifying, filling, and delicious. Sautéed potatoes for breakfast really do fill you up (until lunch!). Use good quality potatoes, good olive oil, fresh herbs and scallions and you can't go wrong.

3 tablespoons extra-virgin olive oil
4 large boiled potatoes, cut into ¼-inch slices
3 scallions, chopped
sea salt and freshly ground black pepper
1 tablespoon chives, finely chopped

- Warm the olive oil in a large frying pan on medium heat. Just as the oil starts to sizzle, pop in the potatoes. Arrange them in a single layer, sprinkle with the scallions, and season well with salt and pepper.
- Cook the potatoes for 7–8 minutes, turning occasionally. Season again with more pepper, sprinkle with the chopped chives, and cook for another minute until the potatoes are golden and crispy. Serve immediately.

**MAKES 4 SERVINGS**

# Pancakes with
# Sweet Honey and Bitter Lemon

OUR recipe is very similar to a "normal" recipe for pancakes, we've just modified and replaced some of the ingredients. This is a good lesson if you find a recipe that looks appealing: just replace the things you can't have with things you can and the original flavor can usually be easily replicated. Try our pancakes, which are healthy and tasty, and see if you can spot the difference! I think lemon and honey make the best topping, though you can try thinly sliced banana and honey or carob spread—a chocolate replacement, suitable for everyone, smeared over the pancakes. Delicious!

1¼ cups white spelt or organic wheat flour
2 free-range eggs
1½ cups rice, oat, soy, goat's, or cow's milk
2 tablespoons bio-live natural yogurt
1 teaspoon organic butter or sunflower oil
3–4 tablespoons local organic honey
1 lemon, cut into wedges

- Put the flour into a mixing bowl. Make a well in the center, add the eggs. Gently mix, then slowly add the milk and yogurt, mixing with a balloon whisk. Keep gently whisking until a batter has formed. Let the batter stand for half an hour if you have the time.
- Put a nonstick pan, roughly 8 inches in diameter, over high heat. When the pan is hot, put a knob of organic butter or drizzle of sunflower oil into it.
- Pour a ladleful of the batter onto the pan and swirl around until you have a pancake shape. Loosen the edges of the pancake with a knife. Cook for 2–3 minutes until bubbles form, then flip over and cook on the other side for another 2–3 minutes. Take the pancake off the heat and keep in a warm place.
- Put another knob of butter or drizzle of oil into the pan and continue with the rest of the batter. Serve the pancakes with a tasty local honey and wedges of lemon.

**MAKES 4 SERVINGS**

# Appetizers, Snacks, Sandwiches, and Accompaniments

Although you can no longer fuel your frantic lifestyle with frantic food, while you adjust from one state of eating to another you will need—if you are to stick to the new regime—loads of tasty snacks to support your body and your mind. Practically all the recipes in this section are interchangeable. Most will make a gorgeous starter classy enough to serve to friends, an excellent snack when you are starving, and a delicious sandwich or an accompaniment when you need a feast.

These are the recipes that will get you through.

# "Sun"-dried Tomatoes

*W*HAT does the image of sun-dried tomatoes conjure up? If all it brings to mind are small, leathery tomato halves drenched in vinegar and raw garlic and sold at exorbitant prices, then you have been deceived. Proper sun-dried tomatoes are a treat—chopped up and mixed into pasta dishes, with salads and in sandwiches, they are delicious. They're also great if you're on a diet, as they add a caramelized sweetness to meals. Since we don't have consistently hot sun, here's how to cheat at "sun"-dried tomatoes.

6 fresh, preferably on-the-vine, tomatoes
2 tablespoons extra-virgin olive oil
sea salt and freshly ground black pepper
3 cloves garlic, whole with skins on
few sprigs fresh rosemary and thyme

- Preheat the oven to 325°F.
- Halve the tomatoes and lay them cut side down on a baking tray. Cover with a coat of olive oil, salt, and pepper. Tuck the garlic cloves, rosemary, and thyme between the tomatoes. Then pop into the oven and cook for roughly 1–1½ hours, until they're dehydrated to your taste.
- If you're not going to use them all at once, you can store them in a clean screw-top jar with a few chopped cloves of garlic, some more herbs, and filled to the top with olive oil. Serve as an appetizer with Bruschetta (page 59), a snack with other snacks, as a very tasty ingredient in a sandwich, or as an accompaniment to savory meals.

**MAKE 12 TOMATOES**

# Slowly Roasted Garlic

*G*ARLIC is gorgeous slowly roasted in its own skin, as it turns super sweet and mellow. To release, just press down on the cooked cloves with the back of a fork and the hot, pungent garlic will come out. Serve as an appetizer or as an addition to (literally) any meal, with olive or other bread and some feta cheese. Give each person, for an appetizer, snack, or accompaniment, one half to one bulb of garlic each, depending on the size of both appetite and bulb of garlic.

**2 bulbs of garlic, whole and unpeeled**
**few sprigs rosemary, bay leaf, and thyme**
**½ cup extra-virgin olive oil**
**sea salt and freshly ground black pepper**

- Preheat the oven to 450°F.
- Tidy up the garlic bulbs by removing excess gritty bits, but be careful to leave the corm (the whole entire garlic) and the tightly bunched skins intact.
- Put into a roasting dish with the herbs and drizzle the olive oil over both bulbs. Season with a pinch of salt and lots of pepper. Pop into the oven for 20–30 minutes.
- Serve with a savory bread and a lump of feta cheese.

**MAKES 4 SERVINGS**

# Baked Potatoes

BAKED potatoes, ah yummy baked potatoes—slowly roasted with their skins on, slit open, and served with a pat of butter and sea salt, what could be better. For a more substantial meal, eat with Hummus (page 63), Slowly Roasted Garlic (page 48), and salad.

**6–8 medium-large "old" potatoes, unpeeled, scrubbed, and cut in half**
**2 tablespoons extra-virgin olive oil**
**few sprigs rosemary and bay leaves**
**4 cloves garlic, not peeled**
**sea salt and freshly ground black pepper**
**1 teaspoon organic butter**

- Preheat the oven to 450°F.
- Make sure the potatoes are well scrubbed. Put into a roasting pan with the olive oil, herbs, and garlic. Season with a little salt and lots of pepper. Toss all together so that the potatoes are well coated. Roast for approximately 1 hour—the exact cooking time depends on size, the bigger the potato the longer time it needs to cook. The potatoes are cooked when a knife or skewer slides easily in and the potatoes themselves are beginning to feel soft when you press them gently.
- Serve sliced open with a pat of butter, a sprinkle of salt, and the roasted garlic cloves.

**MAKES 4 SERVINGS**

# Homemade French Fries

*F*RIES, fries, glorious fries, a fine accompaniment to any meal, or delicious as a snack on their own. Just one thing: when you're making fries, use a good sunflower oil. Other oils just aren't worth using, as many contain genetically modified ingredients.

**4 cups good quality sunflower oil**
**6 large potatoes**
**sea salt**

- Make sure you have a heavy pot (it's safer, because it's far less likely to tip over), with a well-fitting lid. Fill the pot two-thirds up with good quality sunflower oil and put on a high heat.
- While the oil is heating, peel the potatoes and slice into wedges, roughly the width of your index finger. Your oil should be hot enough by now. To test it, drop in a wedge of potato—if it sizzles vigorously, the oil is ready.
- Tip the potatoes into the oil, being very careful to avoid any spitting, cook for 15–20 minutes or until golden brown.
- Remove the cooked fries with a slotted spoon to drain on a plate spread with paper towels. Sprinkle with salt, and *voilà*.

**MAKES 4 SERVINGS**

## Cheese and Bacon Fries

Ohhhh! Oww! The food just gets better and better...! This is Luke's delicious fast-food topping for French fries.

**4 pieces organic bacon, chopped**
**4 scallions, chopped**
**dash of olive oil**
**Cheddar cheese (organic if possible) or feta**
**Harissa (page 171) or chili powder**
**sea salt and freshly ground black pepper**

- First, get the fries cooking as above. While they're cooking, put the bacon and scallions in a pan with a dash of olive oil. Cook gently on medium heat, until the bacon is cooked through, say 7–9 minutes. Remove from heat.

- When the fries are cooked, dry them in a bowl lined with paper towels. Remove paper towel and top the fries with the cooked bacon and scallions. Grate cheese or add feta directly onto the warm chips. Drizzle with Harissa, or sprinkle with chili powder. Season with salt and black pepper.
- Gently stir to mix all the ingredients together and serve. (For best friends only.)

# Caspo Potatoes

CASPO Potatoes are basically Baked Potatoes (page 49) with a gorgeous filling, fairly rich, extremely tasty, and good for cold evenings. We tend to eat them by themselves, perhaps with a salad to fill in the corners.

6 large potatoes, scrubbed
4 bay leaves
2 tablespoons extra-virgin olive oil
sea salt and freshly ground black pepper
2 free-range eggs
2 cloves garlic, peeled and crushed
4 chunks your favorite cheese (we use sheep's)
2 teaspoons organic butter
4 slices prosciutto, chopped

- Preheat the oven to 450°F.
- Put the potatoes, bay leaves, and olive oil in a roasting tray, season with salt and pepper, and toss to coat the potatoes. Place the tray in the oven and cook for 1 hour.
- While the potatoes are cooking, prepare the filling: Break the eggs into a large bowl, add the garlic, cheese, butter, and prosciutto. Season with salt and pepper and mix together.
- When the potatoes are cooked, take the tray out of the oven, cut the potatoes in half and scoop out the flesh, being careful not to damage the skins.
- Add the potato flesh to the bowl and mix everything together. Scoop the mixture back into the potato skins. Push the potato halves back together, return to the oven with Toasted Pumpkin Seeds, and roast for another 5–10 minutes. Serve with a Green Salad (page 68).

**MAKES 4 SERVINGS**

# Tuna, Mayo, and Cucumber Sambos

TUNA and mayo sandwiches are so good, we used to eat them all the time when we were little. The first summer we grew cucumbers, we had to find a delicious way of using them. Then Chupi's boyfriend's little sister, Tara, came up with this great idea—the cucumber reduces the oiliness of the fish, and with homemade mayo you'll want to eat more and more. . . .

**The Mayonnaise:**
½ cup extra-virgin olive oil
¼ cup sunflower oil
1 egg yolk of free-range egg
a good squeeze fresh lemon juice

1 can tuna in sunflower oil
1 small cucumber, chopped
4 scallions, finely chopped
sea salt and freshly ground black pepper
4 Farls, cut in half (page 156)
2 handfuls salad leaves

- For the mayonnaise, combine the two oils, then get a small bowl and put the egg yolk into it.
- Start by adding the first drop of oil, gently mixing it into the yolk. Add the second drop and mix in, always making sure to combine the last drop of oil before adding the next. Slowly increase the amount of oil, but be careful and don't add too much at a time or it will curdle.
- When the egg has absorbed all the oil, add the lemon juice. Season with salt and pepper to taste.
- Now combine the mayo, tuna, cucumber, and scallions in a bowl and mix gently but thoroughly. Season with a pinch of salt and lots of black pepper.
- Divide the mixture into quarters and spread over each half Farl. Add some salad leaves to each sandwich, pop on the tops, season again, and eat.

**MAKES 4 SERVINGS**

# Panzerotte

*P*ANZEROTTE are so versatile, they fulfill all parts of this section: they can be served as an appetizer, a snack, or a sandwich and are especially good for picnics, as everything is sealed tight. Pulled apart, they emit wonderful smells of whatever delicious filling you've chosen, but make sure that the filling is good and intense, with loads of herbs, spices, olive oil, salt, and pepper.

**½ cup white spelt or organic wheat flour**
**½ teaspoon wheat-free baking powder**
**1 tablespoon bio-live organic natural yogurt**
**½ tablespoon your chosen herbs, chopped**
**2 tablespoons extra-virgin olive oil**
**sea salt and freshly ground black pepper**

## The Filling:
**organic feta cheese**
**rosemary, chopped, or Spinach Frittata (page 55)**
**organic soft cheese, or zucchini mixture from Zucchini Pasta (page 91)**
**organic goat cheese, or very ripe tomato, chopped**
**prosciutto or cooked bacon, chopped**
**hard organic cheese, grated or Feta and Sage Relish (page 167)**

- Preheat the oven to 450°F.
- Mix the flour and baking soda in a bowl. Add the yogurt and enough water to make a dry, pliable dough. Split the dough into 6 pieces and roll each into a squarish circle not more than ¼-inch thick.
- Put a large tablespoon of your chosen mix of ingredients into the middle of each circle, season generously, and add some chopped-up herbs—basil and rosemary are our favorites—and a good drizzle of extra-virgin olive oil.
- Fold each circle in half and pinch the pastry together to form half-moons. Glaze with more olive oil.
- Put into the oven for 10–15 minutes or until the parcels are golden brown. Serve with a Green Salad (page 70).

**MAKES 6 SERVINGS**

# Spinach Frittata

*J*F Sunday morning arrives and you're looking for a tasty brunch, look no further. Frittata are Italian omelets and you can fill them with anything you like. They look pretty impressive too, while being extremely simple to make. They can be served as an appetizer, a snack, or with a Green Salad (page 70) as a main meal. And they are a great way to get reluctant spinach eaters started.

**14 ounces spinach**
**1 teaspoon organic butter**
**2 tablespoons extra-virgin olive oil**
**6 tomatoes, chopped**
**6–8 organic free-range eggs**
**2 chunks organic feta goat's cheese**
**sea salt and freshly ground black pepper**

- To sauté the spinach: put the spinach, butter, and 1 tablespoon of the oil into a saucepan over medium heat with a pinch of salt and lots of pepper. Stir to make sure the spinach is coated, put on the lid, and leave for 4 minutes. Stir again. Now continue cooking until the spinach has reduced by roughly half (this should take 8 minutes at the most).
- Meanwhile, place the tomatoes and 1 tablespoon of the oil into a small, heavy-bottomed frying pan or saucepan. Cook over medium heat for 4–5 minutes, stirring occasionally. The tomato and spinach should be done at about the same time.
- Put the tomato to one side while you cook the frittata. Method one: heat a medium-sized, heavy-bottomed frying pan. Drizzle with olive oil and add the beaten eggs. Allow to set (roughly 30 seconds). Now spread the spinach over the egg mixture and allow to cook until the egg is done to your taste (we like ours just firm, about 3 minutes).
- Method two: use a very small, heavy-bottomed frying pan and cook a quarter of the spinach and egg at a time for individual frittatas. Otherwise you can cut the large frittata into quarters.
- To serve, take four pretty plates and put one frittata or one quarter of the large frittata onto each plate and top with one quarter of the fried tomato and a chunk of cheese. Season generously.

**MAKES 4 SERVINGS**

# The Perfect Goat's Cheese, Salad, and Tomato Sandwich

*I*T'S so simple to make a sandwich—just stuff lots of yummy ingredients between two pieces of bread and chow down. But when you can't eat wheat or yeast it is absolutely impossible to get a decent sandwich: sourdough is too bitter and soda bread just crumbles. That's why I urge you to try our Farls (page 156)—they make truly fantastic sandwich bread. If you can't tolerate cheese of any sort, try this sandwich with either Mayonnaise (page 168) or a few slices of ripe avocado as a replacement.

2 Farls (page 156) or 4 pieces bread
1 tomato, very thinly sliced
a few very thin slices red onion
2 large chunks hard goat's cheese, or your favorite organic cheddar, sliced
8–10 green salad leaves
extra-virgin olive oil
sea salt and freshly ground black pepper

- Slice the Farls in half and lightly toast. Meanwhile, prepare the tomato and onion.
- Split the filling between the two sandwiches. Start with a layer of cheese, then the tomato, then the onion. Season generously.
- Drizzle the sandwich with some olive oil and top with the salad leaves and other half of Farl. Eat immediately, or pack up for picnicking later.

**MAKES 4 SERVINGS**

# Quickie Pizzas

THERE'S something about pizza that nothing else quite replicates. But pizza does take a certain amount of work, so here are some Quickie Pizzas perfect as a snack, a quick lunch, or a mid-evening filler. They don't take as much time or energy as normal pizza, but you still get that great pizza hit.

**2 Farls (page 156), sliced open**
**4 very ripe tomatoes, thinly sliced**
**1 red onion, sliced paper-thin**
**enough organic mature cheddar or feta to cover the pizzas**
**2–3 tablespoons extra-virgin olive oil**
**sea salt and freshly ground black pepper**
**1 tablespoon mixed fresh rosemary, basil, and parsley, finely chopped**

- Preheat the oven to 350°F.
- Slice the Farls open to get 4 separate pizzas; pop into the toaster for a minute or two to crisp up.
- On the cut side, layer the tomatoes, then the onion, and then the cheese. Season generously with olive oil, sea salt, and freshly ground black pepper.
- Pop into the oven for 10 minutes. Remove from the oven, sprinkle with fresh herbs, and serve hot. You can serve these as a main meal with a Green Salad (page 70) to fill up the corners.

**MAKES 4 SERVINGS**

## Different toppings

Our favorite pizza is definitely a Margarita, so it's no surprise that the above is topped with a quick imitation of that pizza. You can, however, use other toppings, say 6–8 slices prosciutto underneath the tomato layer for a meat version of the above. You could try Spinach Frittata (page 55) spread across the base, topped with feta cheese or 6 tablespoons crème fraiche, cooked as above. The only limit is your imagination.

# A Mexican Snack: Guacamole and Nachos

*G*UACAMOLE and Nachos are such a classic combination that it seems obvious to join them together as an appetizer or as a snack. We make our own Nachos because it's so simple. One note on the different varieties of avocado: you can usually buy two varieties, the tastiest of which is Hass, with its "warty," nearly black skin. It tastes miles better than its watery green relative.

olive oil
1 quantity Tortillas (page 154) or 1 bag suitable Nachos
1 good-sized, ripe avocado, peeled, pitted, and chopped
1 clove garlic, peeled and crushed
a small squeeze of fresh lemon juice
sea salt and freshly ground black pepper

- You need to make the Nachos first, so put a pan on to warm, cover with a thin layer of olive oil, and get the Tortillas.
- Cut each Tortilla straight down the middle so you have 2 half-moons. Then halve each half-moon so you have four quadrants. Then halve each quadrant so you have 8 triangles in all. You should now have 8 uncooked Nachos per Tortilla.
- The pan should be hot enough by now, so pop 1 Tortilla worth of Nachos onto the pan and fry for a minute or 2 each side or until golden. Remove to drain on paper towels. Continue with the rest of the Tortillas.
- Meanwhile, roughly mash the chopped-up avocado, garlic, and small squeeze of lemon with a fork. We like Guacamole quite chunky, but some people prefer a more puréed consistency; try both and you'll find the consistency you prefer. Season generously.
- Serve as a dip with the Nachos and perhaps some Zingy Tomato Salsa (page 170), as part of a group of salads, or as an element of a sandwich filling.

**MAKES 4 SERVINGS**

## Grown-up Guacamole

Guacamole is suitable for everyone as served above, but if you want to liven it a bit you can add 1 very ripe tomato, finely chopped, and 2 scallions, finely chopped, to the recipe. Serve as above.

WHAT TO EAT WHEN YOU CAN'T EAT ANYTHING

# Bruschetta

*W*ITH all the dips in this section, it's important to have something good to eat them with. Bruschetta are the perfect solution. A sort of upscale fried bread, bruschetta are goldenly crisp and perfect for scooping up Hummus, Avocado Hummus (both page 63), or Guacamole (page 58). Bruschetta are traditionally made with a white yeast bread, but we've used brown soda—both store-bought and homemade—with success. However, if you want to be both Green and traditional, use a white spelt or organic wheat sourdough. You can up the quantities if it's for a big feed or for a party, but these quantities will serve four people as a robust appetizer.

**4 slices bread of your choice (see Excellent Breads pages 151–163)**
**3 cloves garlic, crushed**
**2 tablespoons extra-virgin olive oil**

- Lightly toast the bread.
- Rub both sides of the toasted bread with the crushed garlic and olive oil.
- Presentation is everything, so you can either serve the Bruschetta piled on a plate with bowls of Hummus, Avocado Hummus, and Guacamole with some crudités (such as carrots or celery cut into pretty sticks for dipping and to contrast with the Bruschetta). Or you could cut each Bruschetta in half, pile each half with your chosen dip, and top with a suitable garnish.

**MAKES 8 PIECES**

# Lemon Millet Tabouleh

*M*OST taboulehs are made with couscous. Couscous is not in fact a grain, but rolled wheat, which is not very good if you're wheat-intolerant. Millet is a wonderful grain, acceptable for people who are wheat- and even gluten-intolerant. Try this tabouleh as a tasty snack, appetizer, or accompaniment to a meal with a large salad, as a pasta replacement, or with a chicken breast as a main meal.

¾ cup millet
1¼ cup Veggie Stock (page 77)
1 tablespoon flat-leaf parsley, chopped
3 scallions, finely chopped
3 tablespoons extra-virgin olive oil
2 tablespoons lemon juice, fresh
2 cloves garlic, peeled and crushed

- Put the millet and stock into a saucepan with a tight-fitting lid.
- Cook on a medium heat for 15–20 minutes or until the millet is cooked and fluffy.
- Mix with the rest of the ingredients and serve warm or cold.

**MAKES 4 SERVINGS**

WHAT TO EAT WHEN YOU CAN'T EAT ANYTHING

# Japanese Tempura Vegetables

TEMPURA are vegetables in batter, deep-fried. It may sound bizarre, but tempura is so good—the veggie is gorgeous, crisp on the outside, sweet on the inside. This is an excellent way to encourage vegetable eating. We eat tempura with something simple, but remember to include plenty of dips, perhaps Aioli (page 168), Harrisa (page 171), or Guacamole (page 58). Tempura can serve as an appetizer, snack, or whole meal, provided you have a mix of salads alongside. Gram flour is a wonderful flour, made from chickpeas and suitable for celiacs, so make an effort to find it (try your local health food store). For the vegetables, you can also include whatever is in season.

sunflower oil for deep frying
10 sprigs broccoli, broken into florets
2 carrots, topped and tailed, unpeeled if organic, cut into sticks
8 runner or green beans, topped, tailed, and halved
1 small zucchini, cut into 1-inch sticks
1 cup chickpea flour
½ cup water
white of 1 free-range egg, beaten until fluffy
sea salt and freshly ground black pepper
ground cumin and coriander (optional)

- Put the oil into a pan and heat over a medium-high flame. Prepare the vegetables.
- For the batter: mix the flour and water, whisk to remove any lumps, then gently fold in the egg white. Season with a pinch of sea salt and lots of pepper. You can add 1 teaspoon each ground cumin and coriander if you want to spice it up. Chuck all the veggies into the batter. Mix well, ensuring it's all well coated.
- The oil should be hot by now, so put roughly half the veggies into the oil. Cook for 5–6 minutes, stirring once or twice, until lightly golden. Remove from the oil with a slotted spoon and drain on paper towels. Repeat with the remaining tempura.
- Serve immediately with plenty of dips.

**MAKES 4 SERVINGS**

# Onion Bhajis

ONION Bhajis are another triumph of India's extraordinary culinary classics, but beware, they are quite intense and not to be gorged on if your system is sensitive. As a snack or appetizer with a few dips, or as an accompaniment to an Indian meal, they're supreme. A small tip when cooking: remember always to use a good oil; we use sunflower.

**a saucepan filled with 4 cups of sunflower oil**
**1 cup chickpea flour**
**½ teaspoon each cumin, fennel, black mustard, and coriander seeds,**
    **coarsely crushed**
**½ cup water**
**1 onion, peeled and finely chopped**
**1 potato, peeled and grated**
**sea salt and freshly ground black pepper**
**1 teaspoon each ground cumin, ground coriander, and turmeric**

- Heat the oil over a medium-high flame while you prepare the recipe.
- Combine the flour and all of the spices in a bowl. Slowly add the water to make a smooth batter, then add the prepared onions and potato. Season generously and mix well.
- Drop one tablespoon or more of the thickish mixture into the hot oil, depending on the size of your saucepan. It's fine if the Bhajis bump together as they cook, but you don't want them so tightly packed that they form one big goo.
- Cook for 5–8 minutes until golden brown. Remove and drain on paper towels. Repeat until all the mixture is used.

**MAKES 6–8 BHAJIS**

# Two Different Hummus

**W**E provided recipes for two different kinds of Hummus here, because each is delicious in its own way. Original Hummus is absolute heaven when made properly. A bowl of Hummus and a few Bruschetta—give me five minutes and there will be nothing left! Avocado Hummus is Original Hummus with the addition of an avocado.

**1 pound chickpeas**
**2 cloves garlic, peeled and crushed**
**a small squeeze of fresh lemon juice**
**1 tablespoon mild tahini**
**sea salt and freshly ground black pepper**
**pinch of cayenne pepper**
**Nachos, Bruschetta, crudités**

- Just blend the first 4 ingredients to a roughish consistency and scrape out into a pretty bowl. Season generously and garnish with a pinch of cayenne pepper.
- Serve as a dip, appetizer, or sandwich filling with Nachos (page 58), Bruschetta (page 59), or crudités.

**MAKES ABOUT 10 OUNCES**

## Avocado Hummus

Add 1 good-sized ripe avocado, peeled and pitted, just before you blend the Original Hummus. Serve as above.

# Chili-Cheese Sandwich

THIS is Luke's recipe, so when we debated whether or not it should be a one- or two-person affair, he had the deciding vote: "It's so damn good you could cook for two and eat it alone." So here it is, Luke's version of the traditional grilled cheese sandwich with a new twist. Luke thinks this recipe is best served with a glass of beer, or failing that a glass of apple juice. On the subject of bread, we use homemade, but shop-bought is OK if you can tolerate dairy and wheat. Or you could use your favorite bread, provided it meets the Green requirements. You can also eat these without the bacon, though Luke would not approve.

1 tablespoon extra-virgin olive oil
3 pieces of bacon, cut into strips
4 scallions, chopped
2 slices bread, ¼-inch thick (see Excellent Breads pages 151–163)
organic mature cheddar or feta (to cover bread)
1 large or 2 small very ripe tomatoes, sliced
1 teaspoon Harissa (page 171) or other chili sauce
freshly ground black pepper

- Heat a frying pan over a medium flame with a dash of olive oil. Fry the bacon and scallions for 7–8 minutes, or until browned.
- Meanwhile, lightly toast the bread. Cover with cheese, sliced tomato, and a sprinkle of chili. Season each slice with lots of pepper (no salt is necessary, as the bacon will provide the flavor).
- Pop the toast under the grill until the cheese has melted and the tomato is soft, around 5–6 minutes. Remove, divide the cooked bacon between the two slices, and dribble a teaspoon of Harissa over each.
- Serve immediately with a Green Salad, if you want to make a meal of it. Mouth-wateringly delish!

**MAKES 2 SERVINGS**

# Salads

There is nothing more scrumptious than a good salad, the perfect accompaniment to any meal, reaching every single cell in the body. For Green salad, grow your own in window boxes, visit your local country market, find your local organic farm, do whatever it takes to get good leaves—these are the heart of your salad. Unless, of course, you're trying one of our tasty bean salads. Either way, salads are an excellent companion to all meals or a good stand-alone snack.

# Caesar Salad with Smoky Chicken

THIS recipe came about when after preparing and cooking the separate parts of Chicken Sandwiches (page 132) we decided we wanted something more green! So we put the chicken and mayo into a serving bowl with loads of salad leaves and a chunk of bread to mop up the juices. This is a somewhat complicated recipe, but it's so divine and looks so good it's worth it.

### The Chicken
2 tablespoons extra-virgin olive oil
4 scallions, chopped
3 good-sized chicken breasts, sliced into ½-inch strips
2 cloves garlic, peeled and crushed
1 tablespoon fresh rosemary and parsley, chopped
sea salt and freshly ground black pepper

### The Salad
½ head of romaine lettuce
a generous selection different lettuces, e.g. oakleaf, lollo rosso
1 scallion, chopped
a chunk organic feta or similar cheese, crumbled
2 tablespoons organic bio-live natural yogurt

### The Dressing
1 free-range egg yolk
½ cup extra-virgin olive oil
a good squeeze fresh lemon juice
½ cup bio-live natural yogurt
sea salt and freshly ground black pepper

- Put the chicken ingredients into a large frying pan over medium heat and season generously. The chicken will take about 12–15 minutes, with occasional stirring to prevent sticking, but if you keep an eye on it you can let it do its own thing while you prepare the salad and dressing.
- For the dressing, get a small bowl and put the egg yolk into it. Start by adding the first drop of oil, gently mixing it into the yolk. Add the second drop and mix in again, making sure to combine the last drop of oil before adding the next. Slowly increase the amount of oil, but take it slowly or it will curdle. When the egg has absorbed all the oil, add the

lemon juice and yogurt. Season with salt and pepper to taste.

- The chicken should be just cooked, so pop it into a serving dish on the table along with the salad ingredients and the dressing and mix it all together. A Farl (page 156) or Cheese and Chive Scone (page 158) is an excellent accompaniment to this salad.

**MAKES 4 SERVINGS**

# Mixed Bean Salad
# with Olive Oil Dressing

BEAN salad is another wholefood staple and very tasty. We tend to eat bean salad as part of an array of salads. Originally this would have been made with home-cooked beans, but we feel it's too much work! If you have the time to cook the beans, there is a taste difference, but good canned beans are perfectly acceptable. Bean salad does benefit from being left to marinate for a while.

**1 pound organic mixed beans**
**1 cup bean sprouts**
**½ cup extra-virgin olive oil**
**1 clove garlic, peeled and crushed**
**a good squeeze fresh lemon juice**
**sea salt and freshly ground black pepper**

- Rinse the beans, then toss them with the rest of the ingredients.
- Season generously and serve with Green Salad (page 70) and a Baked Potato (page 49).

**MAKES 4 SERVINGS**

Crunchy Nut Granola (page 37)

Smoothies (page 43). Vanilla—not the runny fast-food kind, the real kind; and strawberry, our favorite.

Fries, fries, glorious (Homemade) fries (page 50)

Caesar Salad with Smokey Chicken (page 66)

"Sun"-Dried Tomatoes (page 47). If there were taste police, "Sun"-Dried Tomatoes would be public enemy number one—they're that good!

Sweet Tomato and Basil Soup with Pesto Crostini (page 79)

Blazing Salads Soup (page 80), probably the best soup in the world

Zucchini Pasta (page 91), the Italian connection

The Ultimate Veggie Burger (page 100). It's hard to believe that paradise comes in pieces this small!

Spelt Pasta with Fava Beans, Tomatoes, and Goat's Cheese (page 96)

Luke and Chupi in Temple Bar food market, Dublin, vegging out

Luke and Chupi scarfing Quickie Pizza (page ii)

# Goat Cheese and Roasted Vegetable Salad

WE first made this recipe as summer was turning into fall and the need for a warm salad—something that seems unthinkable during the summer—emerged. It's very simple: chop up, drizzle, toss in the oven, eat. You can also barbecue the veggies if there's enough sunshine and you have the inclination. Very simple and suitable for everyone, sensitive or otherwise.

6 cloves garlic, unpeeled and whole
2 large very ripe tomatoes, quartered
1 red pepper, deseeded and cut into 12 strips
1 zucchini, halved widthways and cut into thick sticks
few sprigs fresh rosemary, bay leaves
2 tablespoons extra-virgin olive oil
sea salt and freshly ground black pepper
2 scallions, chopped in half
1 handful fresh basil leaves, torn
lots of lettuce and mixed salad leaves
a lump organic feta

- Preheat the oven to 450°F.
- Place the garlic, tomatoes, pepper, zucchini, and herbs into an oven-proof dish. Drizzle with the olive oil and season generously. Pop into the oven and roast for 15 minutes.
- Remove from the oven, add the scallions, and toss. Then put back into the oven for another 10–15 minutes or until the vegetables are cooked.
- Meanwhile, mix the remainder of the olive oil with the basil. When the vegetables are cooked, serve on top of the salad leaves with the crumbled feta on top.

**MAKES 2 SERVINGS**

# Green Salad with Toasted Pumpkin Seeds

*A* GOOD Green Salad is excellent as an appetizer, as an accompaniment to a big meal, or as part of an array of food such as lentil soup (See Blazing Salads Soup on page 80) and a Baked Potato (page 49) for a super-delicious and nourishing meal. A note about buying salad greens: always buy organic, or even better grow your own. Salads can be easily grown in a container indoors or out—and you will know what's happened to your lettuce. Pumpkin seeds with salad might sound strange, but they are delicious, so give them a try!

**1 heaping tablespoon pumpkin seeds**
**½ head of romaine lettuce**
**a generous selection different salad leaves, e.g. oakleaf, lollo rosso**
**a few (5–10) leaves red radicchio (to add color)**

- To toast the pumpkin seeds you can either use the oven or a dry frying pan.
- For the oven: preheat it to 475°F. Put the pumpkin seeds on a tray and pop into the oven for 5 minutes while you prepare the salad.
- For the pan: dry-fry the pumpkin seeds in a frying pan for 4–5 minutes, until lightly browned and crispy.
- Wash the salad leaves well, shake off the excess water, and roughly chop or tear. Put into a serving bowl. When the pumpkin seeds are done, toss them into the bowl with the salad.
- Serve the salad on its own or with a dressing (page 71) as a stand-alone snack, appetizer, or accompaniment to a main meal.

**MAKES 4 SERVINGS**

# Basic Salad Dressing

*I*F you've ever read a list of ingredients for the average salad dressing, or tasted the vinegary goo dolloped over wilted lettuce, then you'll appreciate our perky, tasty dressing for your salads or even to pep up your foods. These dressings can also be stored in the fridge for a few days.

**1 cup extra-virgin olive oil**
**1 tablespoon fresh lemon juice, freshly squeezed**
**sea salt and freshly ground black pepper**

- Pour the olive oil into a jar, add the lemon juice, and season generously with salt and pepper.
- Whisk lightly before serving. Leave it on the table and everyone can drizzle their own.

**MAKES 1 JAR**

## Different Dressings

The **Basic Dressing** is very tasty, but sometimes it's good to have different tastes.

For an **Herb Dressing**, add 1 tablespoon mixed parsley, rosemary, chives, and mint, chopped, to the Basic Dressing.

For a **Honey and Garlic Dressing**, add 1 clove of garlic, crushed, and 2 tablespoons local honey to the Basic Dressing, or to the Herb Dressing.

# Butter Bean, Sun-dried Tomato, and Basil Salad

THIS is our interpretation of a very tasty salad we had in a Dublin restaurant, though without the vinegar. If you have the time to cook the butter beans from scratch, you should—there is a taste difference—but good, organic canned beans are perfectly fine. This is great served with a few other salads, as an accompaniment, or tossed with freshly cooked pasta.

1 pound organic butter beans
6–8 "Sun"-dried tomatoes (page 47), finely chopped
1 tablespoon fresh basil, roughly chopped
1 tablespoon extra-virgin olive oil
1 clove garlic, peeled and crushed
a good squeeze fresh lemon juice
sea salt and freshly ground black pepper

- Rinse the beans well if canned, to get rid of the goo they were preserved in.
- Combine the first 6 ingredients in a pretty bowl. Season with salt and pepper. If possible, leave the salad to marinate for a while.
- Serve at room temperature.

**MAKES 4 SERVINGS**

WHAT TO EAT WHEN YOU CAN'T EAT ANYTHING

# Tuna, Mayo, and Fennel Salad

A TUNA salad is wonderful, so filling and sustaining. This bears no comparison to the normal tuna fish salad, which is made of horrible tuna and cheap mayonnaise; it's a breath of fresh air, with its crisp cucumber and fennel to cut through the mayonnaise. It's not really an accompaniment, but is best served with some crispy bread as a light lunch.

½ cup extra-virgin olive oil
¼ cup sunflower oil
yolk of 1 free-range egg
a good squeeze of fresh lemon juice
sea salt and freshly ground black pepper
1 8-ounce can of tuna in sunflower oil
1 small cucumber, sliced
1 bulb fennel, thinly sliced
4 scallions, chopped
a bowl salad leaves
2 Farls (page 156)

- To make the Mayo combine the two oils. Get a small bowl and put the egg yolk into it. Start by adding the first drop of oil, gently mixing it into the yolk. Add the second drop, mix in again, as usual making sure to combine the last drop of oil before adding the next. When the egg has absorbed all the oil, add the lemon juice. Season with salt and pepper to taste.
- Now combine the tuna, cucumber, fennel, and scallions in a bowl and mix gently but thoroughly. Season again.
- Serve on a bed of salad leaves with some crispy bread—say a toasted Farl.

**MAKES 4 SERVINGS**

# Avocado, Tomato, and Extra-Virgin Olive Oil Salad

*W*ITH some cooking you can afford to not use the best ingredients, but not in salads. Make sure the avocados are ripe, and try to find the Hass variety (nearly black in color). The difference in flavor is incredible. You also need to use on-the-vine tomatoes that are perfectly ripe and a really fruity extra-virgin olive oil.

2 small or 1 large ripe avocado, peeled, pitted, and chopped
2 very ripe tomatoes, chopped
1 scallion, very finely chopped
1 clove garlic, peeled and crushed
3 tablespoons extra-virgin olive oil
sea salt and freshly ground black pepper

- Gently the mix the first 5 ingredients together.
- Season generously with salt and pepper. Serve on its own or as a stand-alone snack, appetizer, or accompaniment to a main meal.

**MAKES 4 SERVINGS**

# Carrot Salad with a Squeeze of Lemon

THIS is a tasty, simple salad, very popular in wholefood restaurants. We eat it with a selection of other salads when we feel like what a friend calls "pure rabbit food."

**3 carrots, peeled and grated**
**1 tablespoon flaked almonds**
**1 large squeeze of fresh lemon juice**
**1 tablespoon extra-virgin olive oil**

- Simply mix all the ingredients together.
- Serve as an accompaniment or with other salads, perhaps a Green Salad.

**MAKES 4 SERVINGS**

# Soups

When you're sensitive, soup is the best food: gentle on the digestive system and yet, if properly prepared, "a meal in a bowl." Using this principle, we recommend extras to serve with the soups for a complete meal; just add or leave out whatever you like. Making your own stock is a must. Most store-bought stock cubes are MSG-, wheat-, yeast-, salt-, and additive-laden, a lethal cocktail for the body. But don't worry, getting a stockpot together is really easy; once you have it up and going, delicious soups will be the order of the day.

# Veggie Stock

THE key to good soups (apart from buying the best and, as much as possible, organic, ingredients) is the stock; a good homemade stock is a must for those of us with food sensitivities. MSG (monosodium glutamate), the flavor enhancer used in most stock cubes and in hundreds of processed foods, is hell on a sensitive system. Making your own stock might seem like a Victorian impossibility—in reality it's easy. The bonus is that once you have a stockpot started, you can just keep adding to it as you go along.

**2 onions (with skin still on) chopped in half**
**1 leek, chopped in half**
**1 large carrot**
**2–3 outer leaves of cabbage**
**2–3 winter/spring greens**
**1 stick celery**
**2 cloves garlic (with skin still on), chopped in half**
**1 bouquet garni (bay leaves/thyme/parsley/sage/rosemary)**
**6 cups water**

- Scrub your vegetables and remove any dirty bits.
- Put them all into a medium-sized saucepan with a tight-fitting lid. Cover in cold water, bring to the boil, and let the ingredients simmer away merrily while you make the soup (a good stock needs a minimum of 30 minutes to get all the flavors from the veggie). Be creative, use whatever veggies are seasonal and at hand. Your stockpot, if kept in a cold place, will last up to 10 days with you adding more vegetables to keep up the intensity of the flavor.

**MAKES APPROXIMATELY 4 CUPS**

# Young Fava Bean
# and Creamy Yogurt Soup

SOUPS are so simple and easy, we tend to live off them during winter when all you want is warm comfort food. However, Fava Bean Soup is best eaten midsummer, when the first tender fava beans are first available, and it can be eaten all the way into early fall. Fava beans are at their best when they're young, but if you can get only the ancient leathery variety, peel the tough gray outer skin after they're cooked—a labor of love, but worth it if you have the time and patience!

1 onion, peeled and chopped
2 cloves garlic, peeled and crushed
1 tablespoon extra-virgin olive oil
3 cups fava beans, de-podded
5 cups Veggie Stock (page 77)
sea salt and freshly ground black pepper
1 tablespoon fresh organic bio-live natural yogurt for garnish
1 tablespoon fresh parsley for garnish

- Sauté the onion and garlic in the olive oil for 6–8 minutes or until soft. Add the beans and cook for 1–2 minutes. Add the stock to the onion, garlic, and beans. (If you want to, you can use a cup of yogurt in place of 1 cup of stock.) Season generously.
- When cooked, blend until smooth. Put the saucepan back on the heat and cook for another 5 minutes to reduce the stock.
- Serve in 4 bowls with a dollop of yogurt and a sprinkle of parsley. This is a very delicate soup, so I'd go without bread, but you could have a Cheese and Chive Scone (page 158) as an accompaniment.

**MAKES 4 SERVINGS**

WHAT TO EAT WHEN YOU CAN'T EAT ANYTHING

# Sweet Tomato and
# Basil Soup with Pesto Crostini

$\mathcal{E}$ VERY recipe we've ever read for tomato soup agrees that without liberal quantities of sugar to counteract the acidity of the tomatoes the soup is not worth making; we disagree! If the soup is properly cooked, the tomatoes release their own flavor, making a very sweet soup. Though we find tomato soup pretty strong, one small
bowl and a heap of Pesto Crostini make a very acceptable meal, especially in the hot
summer.

2 tablespoons extra-virgin olive oil
1 onion, peeled and chopped
1 clove garlic, peeled and crushed
2 8-ounce cans of tomato, chopped
1 cup Veggie Stock (page 77)
1 tablespoon fresh basil
sea salt and freshly ground black pepper
1 quantity Bruschetta (page 59)
½ quantity Green Basil Pesto (page 172)
1 tablespoon organic bio-live natural yogurt

- Warm the olive oil in a heavy-bottomed saucepan over medium heat.
  Sauté the onion and garlic for 5–6 minutes without allowing to brown.
  Add the tomatoes, stock, and basil, stir, and season generously. Let sim-
  mer for 10 minutes.
- A few minutes before the soup is cooked make the Bruschetta. Smear
  each Bruschetta with a large dollop of the Green Basil Pesto to make
  Pesto Crostini.
- Remove the soup from the heat and blend to a smooth consistency.
  Return to the heat, add the yogurt, and warm to serving temperature.
- Serve in 4 beautiful bowls with 2 Pesto Crostini beside each.

**MAKES 4 SERVINGS**

# Blazing Salads Soup

$\mathcal{L}$ENTIL soup, for that is what this recipe is, may not seem all that inspiring, but it is wonderfully gentle comfort food. Very subtle, it's perfect when you are very sensitive. Lentil soup is also great because, stalwart of vegetarians for decades, most meat eaters—who wouldn't normally dream of eating anything veggie—will happily scarf this up! In the notes on this recipe there's attempt No. 1 with the words "Disaster, even the dogs wouldn't touch it" and then attempt No. 2 "Yay!" Here's No. 2, dedicated in loving memory to that gem Blazing Salads, the best alternative restaurant in Dublin and a savior when all other food avenues were dark.

1 large onion, peeled and chopped
2 cloves garlic, peeled and crushed
1 carrot, peeled and chopped
2 tablespoons extra-virgin olive oil
1 cup red lentils
1 teaspoon each ground cumin and coriander
1 tablespoon fresh rosemary and parsley, chopped
5 cups water or Veggie Stock (page 77)
sea salt and freshly ground black pepper
Cheese and Chive Scones (page 158)

- Put the onion, garlic, carrot, and olive oil into a saucepan on medium heat. Sauté for 7–8 minutes without allowing them to brown.
- Now add the lentils, spices, herbs, and stock and season generously. Bring to a boil then reduce the heat. Cover the saucepan with a lid and leave to simmer-cook for 20–25 minutes.
- Now is the time to make the scones. The soup is cooked when the lentils are disintegrating. When it has reached this point, blend until creamy smooth, adjust the seasoning, and serve with your freshly made Cheese and Chive Scones.

**MAKES 4 SERVINGS**

**WHAT TO EAT WHEN YOU CAN'T EAT ANYTHING**

# Allium Soup

THE allium family covers leeks, onions, chives, and garlic, all stuffed with health-giving properties, not to mention their taste-giving properties. And all are included in this delightful soup; soft, sweet, and gentle, it can be eaten by anybody and enjoyed by all.

2 teaspoons organic butter
1 large potato, peeled and chopped
2 onions, peeled and sliced
2 leeks, roots cut off and chopped
4 cloves garlic, peeled and crushed
2 tablespoons extra-virgin olive oil
6 cups Veggie Stock (page 77)
sea salt and freshly ground black pepper
Homemade French Fries (page 50)
Cheese and Chive Scones (page 158)
1 tablespoon organic bio-live natural yogurt
1 tablespoon fresh chives, chopped

- Melt the butter in a saucepan over medium heat.
- Add the chopped potatoes, onions, leeks, garlic, and a healthy dash of olive oil. Toss to ensure everything is well covered. Sauté with the lid on for 9–10 minutes, stirring occasionally to make sure that it doesn't burn.
- When all looks soft and golden, add the stock and season generously. Bring to a boil then reduce the heat and simmer for 20–25 minutes.
- While the soup is cooking make your French Fries or Cheese and Chive Scones. When everything is soft, remove the soup from the heat and blend until completely smooth.
- Serve piping hot with a dollop of yogurt, a sprinkle of chives, and the French Fries or Cheese and Chive Scones.

**MAKES 6 SERVINGS**

# Bacon and Cabbage Soup

THIS is similar to an Italian recipe where a piece of beef is used to flavor a sauce then removed when the sauce is cooked. We take the bacon out before we blend the soup. Bacon and Cabbage Soup is a new twist on that most maligned combination of Irish cooking; don't be put off, just try it. The bacon adds an amazing salty depth to an already tasty soup.

2 onions, peeled and chopped
1 tablespoon extra-virgin olive oil
1 piece organic bacon
freshly ground black pepper
1 small cabbage, sliced
2 cloves garlic, peeled and crushed
1 teaspoon organic butter
6 cups Veggie Stock (page 77)
Homemade French Fries (page 50)
1 tablespoon fresh parsley, chopped

- Sauté the onions with the olive oil in a large saucepan over low heat.
- When the onions have turned pale gold, put the piece of bacon on top and season generously with pepper (there's no need for salt as the bacon provides plenty). Cook for several minutes.
- Now add the cabbage and garlic, topped with the butter. Stir to ensure everything is coated and cook for another few minutes. Then add the stock. Bring to a boil, then reduce and simmer for another 12–15 minutes. If you are making French Fries, now is the time to cook them.
- When the soup is cooked through, remove from the heat and take out the piece of bacon. Blend the soup until smooth.
- Serve with a sprinkle of parsley and perhaps a portion of Homemade French Fries.

**MAKES 4 SERVINGS**

**WHAT TO EAT WHEN YOU CAN'T EAT ANYTHING**

# Mulligatawny (Spicy Chicken Soup)

THIS is the most scrumptious chicken soup you'll ever find. From India (*mulla ga tani*—pepper water), it was a favorite with the British during the days of the Raj. And it is pepper water, hot and spicy, so don't devour the whole pot if you're very sensitive.

1 large onion, peeled and chopped
4 cloves garlic, peeled and crushed
1 tablespoon extra-virgin olive oil
2 good-sized chicken breasts, sliced into ¼-inch strips
4 cardamom pods
4 cloves
1 cinnamon stick
4 curry leaves
12 whole coriander seeds
1 tablespoon ground coriander
1 teaspoon ground cumin
1 teaspoon turmeric
sea salt and freshly ground black pepper
5 cups Veggie Stock (page 77)
Chapati (page 160)
a bowl organic bio-live yogurt

- Gently fry the onion and garlic in the olive oil over medium heat until soft and golden, say 6–8 minutes. Meanwhile slice the chicken.
- Now add all the spices to the onion and garlic mixture. Mix well and cook for several minutes longer. Next, add the chicken pieces and stir again to coat the chicken in the spices. Cook for several more minutes, turning the chicken until browned on all sides. Season generously.
- The last thing to go in is the stock. Then cook on a simmering heat for 30–35 minutes. While the soup is cooking, make the Chapati.
- Once thoroughly cooked and smelling scrumptious, take off the heat, remove the cinnamon stick and liquidize, or serve chunky. Taste. Adjust seasoning. Serve with Chapati on the side and a bowl of natural yogurt. Oh yeah . . .

**MAKES 4 SERVINGS**

# Basic Chicken Stock

CHICKEN soup is definitely food for the soul—and body, and mind—but to get the chicken soup hit, you have to make the stock yourself. Just take the carcass of the chicken you and your loved ones have just devoured, plus any bones left over, put all into a saucepan with lots of nice vegetables (the same ones you would use for Veggie Stock). Bring to a boil and simmer for as long as possible (an hour is about the minimum, 2 to 3 hours is even better).

**1 chicken carcass and bones**
**2 onions (with skin still on) chopped in half**
**1 leek, chopped in half**
**1 large carrot**
**2–3 outer leaves cabbage/2–3 winter/spring greens**
**1 stick celery/several leaves lovage**
**2 garlic cloves (with skin still on), chopped in half**
**1 bouquet garni (bay leaves/thyme/parsley/sage/rosemary)**
**6 cups water**

- Put the chicken carcass in a large saucepan with a tight-fitting lid.
- Scrub the vegetables and remove any dirty bits. Put them all into the pan with the garlic and bouquet garni. Cover with cold water, bring to the boil and let simmer.
- Remove any scum that rises to the surface and allow to cool. Once cool, remove the fat from the surface, and *voilà*, your very own, delicious chicken stock that can be frozen for later use.

**MAKES APPROXIMATELY 4 CUPS**

# French Onion Soup

*F*RENCH Onion Soup is a classic and this version from Bordeaux will have them begging for more. Onions are the most wonderful food, long valued in country medicine for helping to cure everything from colds to rheumatism. This soup rests entirely on the quality of the onions and the stock, so make sure you have the best possible. Organic onions can be bought in most supermarkets and they really are worth eating, unlike their nonorganic counterparts. If you're sensitive to eggs, just leave the egg yolk out.

2 tablespoons extra-virgin olive oil
4 large onions, sliced
2 cloves garlic, peeled and crushed
4 cups Veggie Stock (page 77)
sea salt and freshly ground black pepper
Farls (page 156)
yolk of 1 free-range egg
1 tablespoon chives, chopped, for garnish

- Warm the olive oil over medium heat. Then gently sauté the onions and garlic, with the saucepan lid on, until soft and transparent—be very careful not to let the onions burn.
- After 8–10 minutes add the stock. Season generously, cover again with the lid, and simmer gently for 25–30 minutes. While the soup is cooking, make the Farls.
- When the time is up, remove the saucepan from the heat and liquidize. In a small bowl beat the egg yolk, then slowly add a ladleful of the soup to the egg; go slowly, so you don't curdle it.
- Now pour the egg mixture back into the soup, and mix gently. Warm slowly, not allowing to boil.
- Pour into 4 bowls, garnish with the chives, and serve with a Farl.

**MAKES 4 SERVINGS**

# Cock-a-leekie Soup

"COCK-A-LEEKIE" (cock/hen cooked with leeks) is from Scotland, where they know a thing or two about keeping out winter wet and cold. We make this soup post–Roast Chicken (page 130) when we have all the ingredients on hand—cold chicken and oodles of chicken stock—to make a delightful feast. The key to making this soup delicious is the stock: make your own.

2 onions, peeled and sliced
2 good-sized/4 small leeks, roots cut off, washed, and chopped
1 tablespoon extra-virgin olive oil
1 teaspoon organic butter
sea salt and freshly ground black pepper
6 cups Chicken Stock (page 84)
Farls (page 156)
1 cup cooked chicken meat

- Follow the usual soup-making steps: scrub, peel, and chop your veggies and sauté in olive oil until golden and translucent. Add the butter, the cooked chicken, and season generously. Stir and cook for another minute or so.
- Now add the stock. Bring to a boil, reduce the heat, cover, and cook gently for 15–20 minutes.
- While the soup is cooking, make your Farls. It's up to you whether or not you want the soup liquidized or not. To liquidize, simply blend until smooth. Taste and adjust the seasoning if necessary.

**MAKES 4 SERVINGS**

# Luke's Potato and Carrot Soup

THIS is a wonderful winter soup, gentle on the digestion and delicious to boot.

2 tablespoons extra-virgin olive oil
6 scallions, chopped
4 cloves garlic, peeled and crushed
3 onions, peeled and chopped
1 large potato, peeled and chopped
4 large carrots, peeled and chopped
2 teaspoons butter
sea salt and freshly ground black pepper
6 cups Veggie Stock (page 77)
Homemade French Fries (page 50)
1 tablespoon fresh parsley

- Over medium heat, warm the olive oil. Add the scallions, garlic, and onion. Sauté on a gentle to medium heat for 5 minutes, making sure they don't stick or burn.
- Now add the potato and carrots. Stir well, add one teaspoon of butter, and season generously.
- Next, add the stock and swirl in the second teaspoon of butter. If you're making French Fries, now is the time to put them on.
- Adjust the seasoning. Simmer gently for 15–20 minutes, until all the veggies are really soft.
- Remove from the heat and blend. Serve immediately with a dollop of yogurt, a sprinkle of parsley, and perhaps a Farl or Cheese and Chive Scone (page 158).

**MAKES 4 SERVINGS**

## Libby's Sweet Soup

If after perfecting Luke's delicious Potato and Carrot Soup you want to try a variation, try replacing the potato with I large or 2 small parsnips, peeled and chopped, for a delicious, super-sweet soup. We need to say a big thank-you to the superchef who provided this variation: thanks, Libby!

# Chickpea Soup with Lime Cream

*L*IKE a lot of our soups, Chickpea Soup is heavenly comfort food, perfect when you need to eat simply. However, it can be happily dolled up to suit any occasion with the addition of the lime cream—it gives me a warm feeling just thinking about it! You'll notice this recipe is very similar to Blazing Salads Soup, with a few changes. And a confession: I borrowed the idea of using a lime cream to pep up the soup from another of our favorite books, *The New Cranks Recipe Book* by Nadine Abensur. Thanks!

1 large onion, peeled and chopped
3–4 cloves garlic, peeled and crushed
2 tablespoons extra-virgin olive oil
1 pound cooked chickpeas, junk-free
2 teaspoons each ground cumin and coriander
2 teaspoons cayenne pepper
1 tablespoon fresh rosemary and parsley, chopped
5 cups water or Veggie Stock (page 77)
sea salt and freshly ground black pepper
Cheese and Chive Scones (page 158)
2 tablespoons organic bio-live natural yogurt
1 lime, juiced
a pinch cayenne pepper

- Sauté the onion, garlic, in the olive oil in a saucepan over medium heat for 7–8 minutes without allowing them to brown.
- Now add the chickpeas, spices, herbs, and stock. Season generously, bring to a boil, then reduce the heat. Cover the saucepan with a lid and leave to simmer for 20–25 minutes.
- Now you can make your scones. Also, make the Lime Cream by mixing the yogurt and lime juice.
- The soup is cooked when the chickpeas are disintegrating. When the soup has reached this point, blend until creamy smooth. Adjust the seasoning and pour into 4 bowls. Serve with a dollop of the lime cream on top, a sprinkle of cayenne pepper, and the Cheese and Chive Scones.

**MAKES 4 SERVINGS**

WHAT TO EAT WHEN YOU CAN'T EAT ANYTHING

# Pasta Dishes

There's something about pasta: life just isn't quite the same without it. Like bread, pasta is one of those things that pre-allergies will (probably) have been a major part of your diet. Post-allergies you will probably find it hard to find a pasta that's tasty. We've tried all the alternative varieties, but the only one we have found that tastes—and behaves—like normal pasta, is spelt; we now always eat spelt out of preference. If you are gluten intolerant use millet. So welcome back to the world of pasta! All our pasta dishes can be pulled together in under half an hour, making them the ultimate fast food—in fact just what fast food should be: quick, tasty, filling, and nutritious.

# Warm Pasta, Spicy Olive Oil, and Salty Cheese Salad

ALTHOUGH Luke would never dream of eating this salad, he was the one who came up with it. This is a very simple dish—herbs, cheese, olive oil, and spicy chili with pasta. Serve with a Green Salad for a light meal.

1 pound spelt or organic wheat pasta
4 tablespoons extra-virgin olive oil
2 cloves garlic, peeled and crushed
4 scallions, peeled and chopped
½ tablespoon fresh rosemary, finely chopped
1 tablespoon fresh basil, chopped
4 chunks organic cheese of your choice (we use feta)
sea salt and freshly ground black pepper
2 tablespoons Harissa (page 167)

- Cook the pasta in a large pot of boiling water until al dente, so it retains some bite, about 10 minutes.
- Meanwhile, warm the olive oil in a heavy-bottomed saucepan. Add the garlic, scallions, and herbs. Sauté for 3–4 minutes, until it is all soft and golden, but not yet browning. Leave to one side while the pasta finishes cooking.
- When the pasta is cooked, drain it, return to the heat and toss with the sauce.
- Remove from the heat, crumble through the cheese, season generously with salt and pepper, and allow to marinate for a few minutes. Now add the Harissa, if you're using it.
- Serve on 4 plates, generously seasoned, with a drizzle of seasoned olive oil.

**MAKES 4 SERVINGS**

# Zucchini Pasta

*H*AVING despised zucchini for years, we tried this recipe and now know what we were missing! Pay very close attention the first time you cook this recipe—the zucchini have a tendency to be happily cooking, and then wham they are ready and you need to get them off the heat quickly. The leftovers are also wonderful as a cold salad the next day or as an evening snack.

2 tablespoons extra-virgin olive oil
2 zucchini, sliced into slim rounds
sea salt and freshly ground black pepper
½ pound spelt or organic wheat pasta
3 scallions, chopped
1 large clove garlic, peeled and chopped
3 tomatoes, chopped
1 tablespoon fresh parsley and basil, torn
a piece of lemon

- Take a large frying pan, place over medium heat, and add half the olive oil.
- When the oil has warmed up, add the zucchini, a pinch of salt, and a few shakes of black pepper. The zucchini need frequent stirring to prevent scorching.
- Once the zucchini have been on for 7 minutes and are starting to soften, put the pasta on. The zucchini are cooked after another 5 minutes or so, when they're starting to turn pale golden brown and look caramelized.
- Now add the scallions, garlic, and tomatoes and season generously with salt and pepper. Cook for a few minutes more or until the tomato is perfectly soft, then add the cooked and drained pasta and the herbs. Squeeze the piece of lemon over it all.
- Serve at once or allow to cool and eat as a salad.

**MAKES 2 SERVINGS**

# Spaghetti Bolognese

SPAGHETTI Bolognese makes a good, filling meal, perfect for feeding empty people. It is also idiot proof, just cook it thoroughly. It is very simple for the times when you need to cook on autopilot. If you are vegetarian or vegan, replace the organic chopped beef with the same weight organic tofu, for an equally gorgeous Bolognese.

2 onions, peeled and chopped
3 cloves garlic, peeled and crushed
2 tablespoons extra-virgin olive oil
½ pound organic chopped beef
2 8-ounce cans tomatoes, chopped
½ tablespoon fresh basil, finely chopped
sea salt and freshly ground black pepper
1 pound spelt or organic wheat pasta
sprinkle of cheese (optional)

- Sauté the onions and garlic in the olive oil for 5–6 minutes, until the onion becomes soft and transparent. Add the beef and mix around to coat in the oil. Cook over medium heat for 4–5 more minutes or until the beef is lightly browned.
- Chuck in the tomatoes, basil, and another dash of olive oil. Season generously. Mix it all together and let simmer for about 20 minutes.
- After the sauce has been on for 15 minutes, start the pasta. Cook the pasta in a saucepan full of boiling water on a simmering heat. The pasta and sauce will both finish cooking at around the same time; use your judgment, but the pasta will take about 8–10 minutes.
- Drain the pasta and serve immediately with the sauce on top, perhaps with a drizzle of olive oil and a sprinkle of cheese.

**MAKES 4 SERVINGS**

## Spicy Spaghetti Bolognese

We love Spaghetti Bolognese as it is but Luke disagrees; apparently it's too wimpy! If, like Luke, you prefer your food to bite back, try adding ½ teaspoon chili or cayenne powder, ½ teaspoon ground cumin, and ½ teaspoon ground coriander to the above recipe when you add the beef.

# Bacon Sauce with Pasta

BACON sauce is for those who cannot resist having some form of meat in everything they eat. This dish is a hot and spicy tummy warmer.

2 tablespoons extra-virgin olive oil
4 slices of bacon, cut into strips
sea salt and freshly ground black pepper
3 cloves garlic, peeled and crushed
4–5 scallions, chopped
1 onion, peeled and chopped
2 8-ounce cans of tomatoes, chopped
1 large tomato, roughly chopped
6–8 leaves fresh basil
2 teaspoons chili powder
1 teaspoon ground turmeric
1 pound spelt or organic wheat pasta
a sprinkle of cheese for garnish

- Put a pan onto a medium heat and add a splash of olive oil to the bottom. Throw in the bacon, stir, and season generously with salt and pepper.
- After 2–3 minutes, add the garlic, scallions, and onion. Cook for 5–6 more minutes over medium heat. Then add the canned tomatoes, tomato, basil, chili powder, and ground turmeric. Stir, put the lid on the pan, and let cook for 10 minutes. While the sauce cooks, put the pasta on.
- Bring a pan of water to the boil, add the pasta, and cook for 10 minutes.
- Drain the pasta and take the sauce off the heat. Put the pasta on a plate and add the sauce.
- Season well and serve at once with a sprinkle of cheese.

MAKES 4 SERVINGS

# Spaghetti alla Carbonara

*Y*OU know those days when you just *have* to have something cream-laden? So here we present a Green Spaghetti alla Carbonara. As with a lot of our recipes, this is a classic dish Green-ified, with a gorgeous, creamy sauce and salty bacon strips. Serve with a Green Salad to cut through the creamy pasta. Or not ...

**1 pound spelt or organic wheat pasta**
**5 slices bacon**
**½ cup extra-virgin olive oil**
**yolks of 2 free-range eggs**
**½ cup organic bio-live natural yogurt**
**1 tablespoon fresh basil and parsley, finely chopped**
**2 cloves garlic, peeled and crushed**
**½ cup organic cheddar cheese or feta**
**sea salt and freshly ground black pepper**

- Cook the pasta in a large saucepan with lots of boiling water and a pinch of salt. As the pasta will take about 10 minutes over medium heat, you have plenty of time to prepare the sauce.
- Start by frying the bacon with a splash of olive oil for 5–6 minutes or until golden brown. Meanwhile make the saucy part—a version of mayonnaise.
- Start by adding a drop of olive oil to the egg yolks, gently mixing it into the yolks with a small whisk. Add the second drop, then mix in again. Always make sure to combine the last drop of oil before adding the next. Slowly increase the amount of oil, but be careful or the mixture will curdle. Once the egg yolks have absorbed all the oil, leave to one side while you get the pasta.
- When the pasta is cooked, drain it, then return to the saucepan. Add a splash of olive oil and "dry-out" most of the wet, for about 30 seconds. Turn off the heat.
- Add the mayo to the pasta and stir to coat the pasta. Whatever you do, don't turn your back on the heat, you don't want scrambled eggs!
- Now cut the bacon into thin strips and add the yogurt, basil, parsley, cooked bacon, cheese, and 2 cloves of peeled, crushed garlic. Stir again and season generously.
- Serve immediately, with a Green Salad.

**MAKES 4 SERVINGS**

# Green Basil Pesto with Pasta

*P*ESTO from jars is so nasty it's worth making your own just to see what it should taste like. Pasta with Pesto is a classic combination, a simple, sophisticated dinner that will take ten minutes to prepare. Or if you happen to have a jar of our wonderful Green Basil Pesto (page 172) pre-made, then this will take only as long as the pasta needs to cook. To save time, you don't have to toast the pine nuts, though considering it's going to take the pasta time to cook, you might as well.

1 cup pine nuts
1 pound spelt or organic wheat pasta
2–4 handfuls fresh basil
3 tablespoons extra-virgin olive oil
1–2 cloves garlic, peeled and crushed
1 large lump feta cheese
a squeeze of fresh lemon juice
sea salt and freshly ground black pepper

- Preheat the oven to 450°F.
- Spread the pine nuts out on a baking sheet and pop into the oven for 10–15 minutes or until they are golden brown. Meanwhile, cook the pasta in a large pot of boiling water until it's al dente, say 8–10 minutes.
- Continue with the pesto. You have a choice for making the pesto: a blender, or a mortar and pestle. If using a mortar and pestle, chop up the basil then chuck in and crush all the ingredients except the cheese in your mortar. If using a blender, mix the ingredients together. The consistency is up to you—we prefer to use a mortar and pestle, as you get a rougher, chunkier pesto, but some people prefer a smoother, more store-bought consistency. Try both, see what you prefer.
- When the pasta is cooked, drain and mix pesto and cheese in a large serving bowl. Season generously with salt and pepper and serve immediately.

**MAKES 4 SERVINGS**

# Spelt Pasta with Fava Beans, Tomatoes, and Goat Cheese

*I*F you have ever read Sophie Grigson's *Organics*, a truly wonderful cookbook, you might be surprised by how similar this recipe is to one of hers. Purely accidental! Chupi was starving one day and spotted fava beans, goat cheese, sun-dried tomatoes, and pasta in the kitchen. She made this dish by flinging them together. Months later she was shocked to discover an almost identical recipe in *Organics*. Thus, this gorgeous, quick, tasty recipe had better be dedicated to Sophie Grigson.

1 pound spelt or organic wheat pasta
2 tablespoons extra-virgin olive oil
1 pound shelled fava beans
20–25 "Sun"-dried Tomatoes (page 47)
2 cloves garlic, peeled and crushed
¼–½ cup organic soft goat cheese
1 tablespoon each fresh basil and parsley, finely chopped

- Put a large pan of water on to boil, and when the water is boiling add the pasta. Leave to cook for 8–10 minutes, until al dente.
- Meanwhile, warm the olive oil over medium heat. Add the beans and cook gently, stirring occasionally, for about 5–6 minutes. Add the tomatoes and garlic. Cook for another minute, then remove from the heat until the pasta is ready.
- When the pasta is cooked, drain and return to the pan. Add the bean mixture, cheese, and herbs.
- Warm up on a gentle heat and serve with a Green Salad.

**MAKES 4 SERVINGS**

# Classic Tomato and Basil Sauce with Pasta

THIS uncomplicated and tasty meal can be pulled together in minutes. Everyone loves pasta with a classic tomato sauce, but it's very hard to find a decent version of it. A lot of people just use sauce out of a jar. You might as well use tomato ketchup—unhealthy and not very tasty. Proper tomato sauce is so simple, it's worth making your own. Many cooks believe you should add sugar to all tomato dishes, but there's no need; tomatoes are very sweet, they just have to be cooked properly. This is perfect summer fodder, served with a Green Salad and perhaps a nice bottle of booze if allowed!

2 tablespoons extra-virgin olive oil
1 large onion, peeled and chopped
2 cloves garlic, peeled and crushed
2 8-ounce cans of tomatoes, chopped
1 cup tomato passata
1 tablespoon fresh basil
sea salt and freshly ground black pepper
1 pound spelt or organic wheat pasta
sprinkle of cheese

- Warm the olive oil in a heavy-bottomed saucepan. Add the onion and garlic and sauté for 5–6 minutes. Add the tomatoes, tomato passata, and basil. Season generously with salt and pepper and let cook for another 15–20 minutes.
- The pasta should go on 10 minutes before you expect the sauce to be cooked. Cook the pasta in a large pot of boiling water until al dente.
- When both the pasta and sauce are cooked, drain the pasta, return to the pan, and allow to dry out for about 30 seconds.
- Chuck in the tomato sauce, toss together, and serve immediately on 4 plates with a sprinkle of cheese and a drizzle of olive oil.

**MAKES 4 SERVINGS**

# Veggie Meals

There are those who believe that unless there's something dead and roasted in the middle of the table, it isn't a meal, though luckily there are lots of the other kind of people as well. This chapter is for them and, while they're scoffing their way through their delicious meal, let them pretend not to notice the hand creeping in from the side, "Do you mind if I just try a bite?" Yes, veggie meals are for everyone, even if you have to compromise and pretend there's something dead in the food! And if you are one of those "if it's not dead it's not edible" types, then please give us an opportunity to convert you, if not to a strictly vegetarian way of eating, to at least the occasional enjoyment of a gorgeous veggie meal.

# Piperade

*A*PPARENTLY in France this tasty dish is served as breakfast. Well, it would make a very tasty breakfast, but you'd need a clear space in which to cook it; try Sunday morning, the perfect day on which to enjoy a large brunch and the news-papers.

**2 tablespoons extra-virgin olive oil**
**1 large onion, peeled and chopped**
**2 cloves garlic, peeled and crushed**
**1 red pepper, deseeded and cut into ¼-inch strips**
**sea salt and freshly ground black pepper**
**5 tomatoes, chopped**
**4 Farls (page 156)**
**4 free-range eggs**

- Warm the olive oil in a heavy-bottomed frying pan. Add the onion and garlic and sauté for 5 minutes over medium heat.
- Now add the pepper. Season generously and cook for another 5 minutes. Then add the tomatoes to the pan and cook for another 10 minutes.
- Make the Farls while the sauce continues cooking.
- When the sauce is ready, make 4 hollows in it and into each hollow break an egg. Cook for 4–5 minutes more or until the eggs are cooked to your liking. Serve each egg with a quarter of the Piperade and a Farl.

**MAKES 4 SERVINGS**

# The Ultimate Veggie Burger and Fries

*F*OR years we tried to make a veggie burger that a) tastes nice; and b) didn't disintegrate on contact with heat. Success at last! We absolutely love these burgers. A word of advice: you must use all the toppings to get the ultimate hit. On the subject of bread, we find Farls to be so perfect and so easy, we always use them. However, if you want to replace them with suitable "Green" bread, go right ahead.

### The Burgers
2 8-ounce cans of cooked chickpeas, drained and blended
1 teaspoon each ground cumin and coriander
1 tablespoon fresh parsley, chopped
4 scallions, chopped
4 cloves garlic, peeled and crushed
3 teaspoon lemon juice, freshly squeezed
1 tablespoon extra-virgin olive oil
sea salt and freshly ground black pepper
1 cup gram flour

### The Buns
3 cups white spelt or organic wheat flour
1 teaspoon baking soda
¾ cup water or rice, oat, soy, or cow's milk
1 tablespoon bio-live natural yogurt

### The Extras
½ cup crumbled organic feta cheese
sea salt and freshly ground pepper
salad leaves
¼ red onion, very thinly sliced
2 tomatoes, very thinly sliced
2 tablespoons Garlic Aioli (page 168)
Homemade French Fries (page 50)
Harissa (page 171)

Peruvian Steak (page 124)

Spiced Chicken Wraps (page 129), delicious and delectable

Luke going to town on the Chili Chicken Dippers (page 134)

We were going to show before and after pictures, but that would have been too depressing!

Chupi eating Brian's Spicy Chicken Curry with Organic Brown Rice (page 126). Ah, isn't love beautiful!

Fish Stew (page 115)

Chapati (page 160), a national treasure from India

Raspberry and Yogurt Fool (page 138): there's no fool quite like a Raspberry Fool!

Indulgence Chocolate Cake (page 148)

Twice-Baked Biscotti (page 137)

A Green Brown Bread (page 161)—the staff of life

Toast

Chili-Cheese Sandwiches (page 64). You haven't lived until you've tasted one of these.

Harissa (page 171): hot flashes all around!

- Get your burgers together first. Blend the chickpeas to a lumpy consistency. Add ingredients and combine with a spoon—if it's too sticky, add a little more flour. Season generously with salt and pepper. There should be enough mix for about 8 burgers—just store whatever you don't need in the fridge.
- Dust your hands with plenty of flour, take 4 handfuls of mix, roll each into a ball, then flatten into burgers about ½-inch thick. Now you can get the fries on.
- Warm half a tablespoon of olive oil in a large frying pan. Add the 4 burgers and cook over medium heat for 4–5 minutes per side or until done to your liking. While the burgers are cooking, make the buns.
- Mix all the bun ingredients together, to form a soft, not too sticky dough. Divide into 4 balls and flatten to ½-inch thick. Put another frying pan on medium heat and sprinkle with flour. When the flour starts to brown, put the buns on for about 4 minutes per side.
- To serve, slice the buns in half, plonk on the burger, add a couple of slices of cheese, a twist of pepper and salt, a few salad leaves, the red onion, the tomato, some Garlic Aioli and some Harissa.
- Serve with French Fries and/or a Green Salad.

**MAKES 4 SERVINGS**

# The Green Margarita

$\mathcal{P}$IZZA is our universal favorite meal. However, most "normal" pizza is poison with the base made from commercial wheat and yeast, the sauce a suspicious tomato and sugar goo. As for the topping? Don't even go there! We've tried numerous recipes to come up with the perfect pizza: a crisp, chewy base, a sweet tomato sauce, and delicious cheese topping. This is definitely the work of four people. We proudly present the Green Margarita. This makes two pizzas—in our opinion just enough for four people.

## The Sauce
1 onion, peeled and chopped
3 cloves garlic, peeled and crushed
2 scallions, peeled and chopped
2 tablespoons extra-virgin olive oil
1 cup tomato passata
1 tablespoon fresh basil, torn
few sprigs rosemary, finely chopped
sea salt and freshly ground black pepper
2 8-ounce cans of tomatoes, chopped

## The Base
3 cups white spelt or organic wheat flour
1 teaspoon wheat-free baking powder
1 teaspoon dried thyme
¾ cup water or rice, oat, soy, or cow's milk

## The Topping
your favorite cheese (we use feta)
6 tomatoes, thinly sliced
1 tablespoon fresh basil, torn
few sprigs rosemary, chopped
sea salt and freshly ground black pepper
1 tablespoon extra-virgin olive oil

- Start with the sauce. Sauté the onion, garlic, and scallions in the olive oil for 5–7 minutes, until soft, on medium heat. While that's cooking, start the base.

- Get a mixing bowl, mix the dry ingredients together, and make a well in the center. Add the milk and mix until it is all absorbed. You should have a soft, not too sticky dough. Give it another knead, then form it into a ball, divide in half, and roll each out into a circle no more than ¼-inch thick. Get out a large frying pan, put it on medium heat, and sprinkle with flour. Back to the sauce.
- Add the can of tomatoes, passata, and herbs to the onions and garlic. Season well with salt and pepper and let cook while you continue with the base. When the flour starts to brown, lift the base onto the pan with the aid of a wooden spoon. Cook each base for 3–7 minutes per side until lightly browned. By the time this is done, the sauce should be perfect.
- Put the bases on 2 circular baking pans. Slather the sauce on top and sprinkle with the cheese. Layer on the slices of tomato, scatter the herbs, season generously, and drizzle the olive oil over it.
- Pop under the grill for about 10 minutes or until the cheese has melted. While the pizzas are finishing, make the Green Salad. Serve immediately.

**MAKES 4 SERVINGS**

# Cianfotta
# (Mediterranean Vegetable Stew)

CHUPI was once so sensitive that the idea of eating sweet peppers made her shudder, but thanks to good food and good work on the health front, she can now enjoy this beautiful combination of sweet Mediterranean vegetables. It's very easy to prepare, as it can be left to stew while you make a myriad of accompaniments. Cianfotta is gorgeous as a vegetable dish or as a main meal with a chunk of bread or some brown rice. As a bonus, it can be eaten cold the next day. Delish. We've also included a recipe variation for Ratatouille.

1 onion, peeled and chopped
3 tablespoons extra-virgin olive oil
6 large very ripe tomatoes, chopped into chunks
1 red pepper, deseeded and cut into ½-inch strips
1 yellow pepper, deseeded and cut into ½-inch strips
1 medium zucchini, chopped into circles ¼-inch thick
6 cloves garlic, peeled and halved
1 handful fresh basil leaves
sea salt and freshly ground black pepper
2 cups short-grain brown rice
4–5 cups water
4 Farls (page 156)

- Sauté the onion in half the olive oil until tender.
- Add the remaining vegetables, garlic, and the remaining olive oil and stir to ensure all the veggies are evenly coated with the oil. Season generously with salt and pepper. Cook over low heat with the saucepan lid on for 40–45 minutes, until the vegetables are soft but not disintegrating. While the stew is cooking, make the Farls.
- Put the rice on when the stew has been cooking for roughly 25 minutes. Put the rice and 4–5 cups of water in a saucepan with a tight-fitting lid and cook over medium heat (it should be cooked at the same time as the stew). Serve the stew on the bed of rice with the torn up basil leaves, perhaps with the Farls.

**MAKES 4 SERVINGS**

# Ratatouille

Cianfotta is the Italian version of that much more famous vegetable stew, Ratatouille. However, for our version of Cianfotta, we don't include eggplant. If you feel like trying a Ratatouille, simply add 1 eggplant, diced, at the same time as the rest of the vegetables. Also, if you want to spice it up and remain true to the original, add 1 teaspoon paprika at the same time as the eggplant. Ta-da! Your Cianfotta is now a Ratatouille.

# Chili without Carne

CHILI without meat? Strange as it may sound, some prefer chili without carne—we use organic tofu instead because it's so good. Of course if you must, you can substitute organic chopped beef, but I can't really see the point, as the result is very similar and it does everyone good to eat veggies, occasionally. We've all tried chili, so there is no need to enumerate the benefits of this hot, tasty dish. There aren't any secrets, except to be careful when you're cooking the tofu, as you don't want it to completely disintegrate.

2 onions, finely chopped
4 cloves garlic, peeled and crushed
1 tablespoon extra-virgin olive oil
1 block organic tofu, cut into ½-inch cubes
2 8-ounce cans of tomatoes, chopped
1 8-ounce can of kidney beans, rinsed
3 teaspoons each ground cumin, coriander, and chili powder
1 tablespoon each of fresh parsley, basil, and rosemary, chopped
sea salt and freshly ground black pepper
1½ cups basmati rice
3½ cups water
1 quantity Nachos (page 58) or
1 quantity Tortillas (page 154) (optional)
dollop organic bio-live natural yogurt (optional)

- Sauté the onions and garlic in the olive oil for 4–5 minutes or until translucent.
- Now add the tofu and stir gently to ensure that it is evenly coated in the olive oil. Allow to cook for another 5–6 minutes until the tofu is lightly browned.
- Then add the tomatoes, beans, spices, and herbs. Season generously with salt and pepper. Bring the chili to a simmer, then reduce the heat, put a lid on the saucepan, and let cook for 30–40 minutes over medium heat. Meanwhile, prepare the Nachos or Tortillas, whichever you have chosen.
- Ten minutes before the chili is cooked, put the basmati rice and water into a saucepan with a tight lid. Cook the rice over medium heat. The rice and the chili will be done around the same time, but keep an eye on both toward the end of their cooking time.
- Serve the chili on the basmati with a dollop of yogurt and the pile of Nachos or Tortillas for the ultimate Latin America-inspired feast.

**MAKES 4 SERVINGS**

**WHAT TO EAT WHEN YOU CAN'T EAT ANYTHING**

# Mom's Spanish Omelet

*W*ITH its scrumptious, fortifying innards, the Spanish Omelet really is eating and drinking. Make sure to get the best eggs you can and that all your ingredients are squeaky-clean fresh. A wonderful dish for any time of the night or day.

1 tablespoon extra-virgin olive oil
2 slices of bacon, cut into strips (optional)
4 scallions, chopped
2 cloves garlic, peeled and crushed
2 very ripe tomatoes, chopped into chunks
4 cold cooked potatoes, chopped into rough ½-inch cubes
1 tablespoon each of basil and parsley, finely chopped
4 Farls (page 156)
4 free-range eggs
sea salt and freshly ground black pepper

- Place a large frying pan over medium heat with a splash of olive oil. If using the bacon, put into the pan while you prepare the rest of the ingredients.
- When the bacon is nearly cooked, add the scallions, garlic, tomatoes, cooked potatoes, herbs, and remainder of the oil. Season with a little salt and generous amounts of pepper. Cook over medium heat, stirring occasionally, for about 8–10 minutes. While the omelet mix is cooking, make the Farls.
- Break the eggs into a bowl, season with salt and pepper, and mix together. Remove the bacon and potato mixture onto a plate. Put the egg mixture into the hot frying pan. Swirl so that the mix covers the base of the frying pan and cook until it's just beginning to set, about 3 minutes.
- Spread the potato mix evenly over the omelet and allow to cook for 2–3 more minutes. Slide the omelet off the pan, divide into 4, and serve each atop a toasted, halved Farl.

**MAKES 4 SERVINGS**

# Kitchiri with Chapati

DHAL from India is one of life's treats. This is the real thing, a genuine Indian dhal served with genuine Indian Chapati. OK, not really, but this is damn close to the real thing.

1 cup green lentils
1 teaspoon organic butter
2 tablespoons extra-virgin olive oil
1 large onion, peeled and finely chopped
2 cloves garlic, peeled and crushed
1½ cups basmati rice
1 teaspoon ground turmeric
1 teaspoon each black mustard, cumin, cardamom, and fennel seeds
3 teaspoons each ground cumin and coriander
3 bay leaves
4 cloves
1 cinnamon stick
4 cups water or vegetable stock
1 cup tomato passata or chopped canned tomatoes
sea salt and freshly ground black pepper
1 quantity Chapati (page 160)
1 tablespoon fresh parsley, chopped
a bowl organic bio-live natural yogurt

- Soak the lentils in enough boiling water to cover them while you prepare the rest of the ingredients.
- Put the butter, olive oil, chopped onion, and crushed garlic into a large saucepan. Sauté gently over medium heat for 5 minutes. Then add the basmati rice, herbs, and spices, mix well, and cook for a few minutes more. When that's done, add the lentils, stock, and passata or tomatoes and season generously.
- Bring to the boil, put a lid on the saucepan then reduce the heat. Cover and simmer for half an hour or until all the stock is absorbed and the lentils and rice are soft but still retaining some "bite." If you're making the Chapati, now's the time to do it.
- When the dahl is cooked, adjust the seasoning to your taste and add the parsley. Serve with the Chapati, a bowl of natural yogurt, and perhaps a Green Salad.

**MAKES 4 SERVINGS**

# Winter Roast Roots

*A*N excellent middle-of-winter dish, the roasting caramelizes the veggies to sweet perfection. We'd normally eat this as an evening meal with a Green Salad for contrast, and lots of dips, say Harissa, Aioli, and Hummus. Vary your choice according to your taste. One question about this recipe is whether or not to peel the vegetables: it's a matter of personal choice, but we generally peel all those that aren't organic and just scrub those that are.

6 potatoes, scrubbed, halved if small, quartered if large
4 carrots, cut in half lengthways
2 onions, not peeled, quartered
2 parsnips, cut in half lengthways
2–3 baby turnips
2 beets, halved
any other root vegetables in season
8–10 cloves garlic, not peeled, whole
few sprigs rosemary
few bay leaves
3 tablespoons extra-virgin olive oil
sea salt and freshly ground black pepper
Green Salad (page 70)
Harissa (page 171)
Aioli (page 168)
Hummus (page 63)

- Preheat the oven to 400°F.
- Put the prepared vegetables and garlic into a large roasting tray. Stuff the herbs in around them and over them. Drizzle with the olive oil, season with a few pinches of salt and lots of pepper.
- Pop into the oven for 45 minutes, turning the veg halfway through the cooking time. While the vegetables are cooking, prepare the Green Salad, Harissa, Aioli, and Hummus.
- Serve with a few chunks of feta mixed through, the Green Salad on the side, and the dips in little bowls.

**MAKES 4 SERVINGS**

# Zucchini and Basmati Tart

*R*EAL men, they say, don't eat quiche. Given the hideous and ubiquitous soggy confection universally sold as quiche, it's surprising anyone does. But banish all thoughts of that quiche from your mind, this little baby, with its sweet crunchy pastry, delicious ingredients, and intense texture will have real people, male and female, begging for more.

**1 cup white spelt flour**
**1 teaspoon organic butter**
**2 tablespoons extra-virgin olive oil**
**1 free-range egg, beaten**
**3 shallots**
**2 cloves garlic**
**2 tablespoons extra-virgin olive oil**
**2–3 zucchini, sliced**
**1 cup basmati rice, cooked**
**2 free-range eggs, beaten**
**3–4 tablespoons organic bio-live natural yogurt**
**few sprigs rosemary, chopped**
**sea salt and freshly ground black pepper**
**Green Salad (page 70)**
**2 chunks organic feta cheese**

- Preheat your oven to 350°F.
- To make the pastry: put the flour into a mixing bowl and rub in the butter until you have a crumbly, bread crumb texture. Make a well in the center and pour in the olive oil, egg, and a splash of cold water if needed. Stir the flour into the liquid, mixing gently until you have a soft dough. Knead for 2–3 minutes. Put the dough in the fridge to rest.
- After about 20 minutes, take the pastry out of the fridge, oil a 7-inch tart pan, and roll the pastry out to fit it. Prick the pastry all over with a fork and pop back into the fridge for another 5 minutes.
- Line the pastry case with parchment paper weighed down with baking beans (any dry beans from your cupboard will do, provided you don't try to eat them afterward!). Put the pastry case in the oven for 20 minutes. Meanwhile, prepare the filling.

- Sauté the shallots and garlic in the olive oil until soft, around 5–6 minutes. Then add the zucchini. Stir and cook for another 15 minutes over gentle heat with the saucepan lid on.
- The pastry case will be ready a minute or so before the filling, so remove it from the oven. Remove the baking beans and paper and return to the oven for another 4–5 minutes to crisp. While the pastry is completing its cooking, prepare the filling.
- Remove the zucchini mix from the heat—it should be nicely cooked by now, soft and sweet. Mash roughly with a fork and allow to cool. Add the remaining ingredients and mix well. Season generously.
- Take the pastry case out of the oven. Pile the filling into the case, smooth down, and drizzle over with olive oil. Bake in the oven for 30–35 minutes until golden.
- When the tart is almost cooked, make the Green Salad. Serve with a crumbling of cheese and the Green Salad. Heaven.

**MAKES 4 SERVINGS**

# Perfect Sautéed Rice

**W**ITHOUT a doubt, in times of hunger, this has been our culinary savior, so simple, healing, and tasty. I wouldn't touch the average fried rice, with its raw, crunchy ingredients and rubbery egg, but this is a delight: sweet tasty vegetables and rice. As with all recipes, experiment—if you're vegetarian, leave out the bacon; if you're a bamboo-shoot nut, add them; if you dislike green beans, substitute broccoli. Just ensure that all your ingredients are tasty and fresh. Fried rice isn't supposed to be all the leftovers in the fridge with rice. We've left the egg optional, as we prefer a gentler rice, but add it if you want something more robust.

2 tablespoons extra-virgin olive oil
1 slice bacon, cut into small slivers (optional)
3 scallions, chopped
2 cloves garlic, peeled and crushed
2 very ripe tomatoes, chopped into chunks
1 handful green beans, chopped into ½–¾-inch bits, or
1 handful broccoli, cut into florets
sea salt and freshly ground black pepper
4 cups cooked short-grain brown rice
1 free-range egg (optional)
2 chunks organic feta cheese

- Place a large frying pan over medium heat with a splash of olive oil. If using bacon, put it into the pan while you prepare the rest of the ingredients.
- When the bacon is nearly cooked, add the scallions, garlic, tomatoes, and green beans (or broccoli). Season with a little salt and lots of black pepper.
- Find a large saucepan lid that neatly covers the pan—this prevents all the tasty juices evaporating. Cook over medium heat, stirring occasionally, for about 8 minutes, until everything is soft.
- Take the pan off the heat, add the rice, and mix together. Then, if you're using an egg, break it into the middle of the rice and mix thoroughly. Put the rice back on the heat and cook for another 2–3 minutes, until the egg is done to your liking; if not, just serve immediately.
- Serve with some feta cheese crumbled through, drizzled with olive oil, and a fresh Green Salad. Our favorite "fast-food" meal.

**MAKES 4 SERVINGS**

**WHAT TO EAT WHEN YOU CAN'T EAT ANYTHING**

# Green Gratin Dauphinoise

S LOWLY, slowly cooked gratin—layer upon layer of potatoes and onions baked in the oven—is a wonderful winter dish. For sensitive stomachs, it doesn't have to be cooked in cream; substitute oat milk, a creamy alternative to dairy milk, and best quality Veggie Stock (page 77).

1 tablespoon extra-virgin olive oil
1 teaspoon organic butter
8 large potatoes, peeled and thinly sliced
1 large onion, peeled and thinly sliced
3 cloves garlic, peeled and crushed
3 scallions, sliced
sea salt and freshly ground black pepper
8 sprigs rosemary, finely chopped
2 cups oat milk
2 cups Veggie Stock
Green Salad (page 70)
crumbled feta cheese

- Preheat the oven to 325°F.
- Grease an ovenproof gratin dish generously with oil and butter. Build up layers of potatoes, onion, garlic, and scallions, seasoning with salt and freshly ground black pepper and scattering with rosemary. Halfway up your gratin dish, pour in a mixture of oat milk and stock up to the level of the potatoes. Then finish off the layers of vegetables.
- Pour in the remaining mixture of oat milk and stock. Bake in the oven lightly covered with parchment paper for 1½ hours, until soft through and through.
- While the gratin is cooking, make the salad. When the gratin is cooked, crumble the feta over the top and serve with the Green Salad. And remember, gratin is even more delicious reheated the next day.

**MAKES 4 SERVINGS**

# Fish Meals

When it comes to eating fish, all we can do is hold up our hands and say, guilty: we don't eat much of it. For the next book we plan to take up an invitation from a long-ago friend who has promised that if we come to an Atlantic hideaway armed with skillet and knife, he will teach us everything there is to know of the glory of cooking and eating fish. That said, Luke's fish stew is absolutely delicious and can be adapted to almost any fish available. His pan-fried fish can also be adapted, so please forgive and, do what we suggest, enjoy!

# Fish Stew

THIS stew is very good to eat for two reasons: it is very nutritious, and it tastes so very good!

2 tablespoons extra-virgin olive oil
2 onions, peeled and chopped
4 scallions, sliced
4 cloves garlic, peeled
1 large cod fillet, cut into cubes
1½ cups shrimp, whole
sea salt and freshly ground black pepper
1¾ pounds chopped tomatoes
½ teaspoon chili powder

- Heat a saucepan containing the oil over a low flame. Sauté the onions slowly. Add the scallions and the garlic and cook, still nice and slow, for 10 minutes, until the onions, garlic, and scallions are all soft and golden.
- Add the cod and the shrimp. Sauté for another few minutes, turning gently so as not to break up the fish. Taste and then season with salt and pepper.
- Add the tomatoes and the chili. Taste again, put on a lid and stew, still nice and gently, for 30 minutes.
- Serve with organic basmati rice and a Green Salad.

**MAKES 4 SERVINGS**

# Fried Fish

*F*OR this delicious recipe, you can use fresh fillets of cod, haddock, or flounder. We usually use haddock, but the choice is yours.

1½ cups white spelt or organic wheat flour
2 tablespoons extra-virgin olive oil
1½ cups water
1 large free-range egg
4 fresh fish fillets
Homemade French Fries (page 50)
4 slices lemon or splash of vinegar
sea salt and freshly ground black pepper

- Sieve the flour into a bowl. Add the olive oil and the water. Whisk to prevent lumps. Gently fold in the egg and leave for half an hour.
- Dip the fish fillets in the batter, making sure that they are covered all over. When your fish is ready to go, start your French Fries.
- Now put the fish in the hot oil and cook for 10–15 minutes or until golden brown. Take them out with a slotted spoon and dry with paper towels.
- If there is any batter left, slice some onion into rings, dip in the batter, and cook in the french fry pan until brown—around 10 minutes.
- Serve the fish with a squeeze of lemon or if you can tolerate it, a little vinegar, and a heaped bowl of Homemade French Fries.

**MAKES 4 SERVINGS**

WHAT TO EAT WHEN YOU CAN'T EAT ANYTHING

# Meat Meals

$\mathcal{L}$et's face it, most men believe that there's no substitute for red meat and Luke believes this passionately too! But increasingly we are being told that with our relatively recent sedentary lifestyle, too much red meat is a bad thing. So keep red-meat eating to a minimum. Make sure every bite is 100 percent delicious, and 100 percent additive free, by trying to buy organic. The taste difference is worth it and the health difference could be a life-and-death one.

# The Classic Burger with Extras

THERE'S something so tasty about a burger in a soft, chewy bun with fresh toppings, no wonder it's so many meat-lovers' favorite meal. It's easy to buy ready-made burgers, but if you've ever read the list of ingredients on one of the packets, you'll understand why it's important—considering it's so simple—to make your own. Make sure to use all the extras for true enjoyment.

### The Burger
3 scallions, finely chopped
1 pound organic chopped beef
yolk of 1 free-range egg
2 cloves garlic, peeled and crushed
sea salt and freshly ground black pepper
½ tablespoon extra-virgin olive oil

### The Buns
3 cups white spelt or organic wheat flour
1 teaspoon wheat-free baking powder
¾ cup water or rice, oat, soy or cow's milk

### The Extras
2 tablespoons Harissa (page 171)
8 slices organic cheese
salad leaves
2 tablespoons Mayonnaise (page 168)
Homemade French Fries (page 50)
Aioli (page 168)

- If you're making Fries, get them on first, so you can keep them warm.
- Mix first 4 burger ingredients together and season generously with the salt and pepper. Split the mix into 4 pieces, roll into balls, then flatten into burgers about ¾ of an inch thick.
- Warm half a tablespoon of olive oil in a large frying pan. Add the 4 burgers and cook over medium heat for 5–6 minutes each side or until done to your liking.
- If you are making buns, mix all the ingredients together to form a soft dough. Divide into 4 balls, and flatten to ½-inch thickness. Put another frying pan on medium heat and sprinkle with flour. When the flour

starts to brown, put the buns on for about 4 minutes per side or until puffed up.

- To assemble, slice the buns in half, spread each half with Harissa, plonk on the burger, add a couple of slices of cheese, a twist of pepper and salt, a few salad leaves, and some Aioli. Serve with Homemade French Fries.

**MAKES 4 SERVINGS**

# Spicy Meatballs in Tomato Sauce

*M*EATBALLS do take a little time to prepare, but they are truly worth it. The spices make this one of the most heart- and tummy-warming dishes you could imagine. If you've stopped eating meat, find a good organic butcher—you can even find one online these days. Yes, the meat is more expensive, but just buy a little at a time and savor the difference. If you can't take meat in any shape or form, substitute red lentils or organic tofu, both of which are available in health food stores. Cook the meatballs carefully, as you don't want them to crumble.

## The Meatballs

1 pound organic chopped beef
yolk of 1 free-range egg
2 teaspoons each ground turmeric and ground chili
2 cloves garlic, peeled and crushed
sea salt and freshly ground black pepper

## The Sauce

2 onions, peeled and chopped
3 cloves garlic, peeled and crushed
2 tablespoons extra-virgin olive oil
2 teaspoons each ground cumin, turmeric, and coriander
2 teaspoons ground chili
2 8-ounce cans of tomatoes, chopped
1 cup tomato passata
sea salt and freshly ground black pepper
2 cups basmati rice
4 cups water
1 cup organic bio-live natural yogurt
Chapati (page 160) (optional)

- For the sauce, sauté the onions and garlic in the olive oil until they are golden. While they are cooking, mix together the first four meatball ingredients, seasoning well with salt and pepper, and making sure everything is thoroughly combined.
- Divide the meat mixture in half, then halve again, then again, then once more. You should end up with 16 pieces. Roll each into a meatball roughly the size of a walnut.

- The onion and garlic mixture should be cooked by now, so put it to one side of the pan and add the meatballs and the spices from the sauce ingredients.
- Cook for 7–8 minutes until the meatballs are nicely browned all over. Now add the tomatoes and passata. Season generously, stirring all the ingredients together very gently so as not to break up the precious meatballs. Cook over a low heat for approximately 40 minutes.
- Ten minutes before the meatballs are cooked, pop the basmati rice and water in a saucepan with a tight-fitting lid and cook over medium heat. If your timing's good, the meatballs and rice should be at the same time.
- Adjust the seasoning of the meatballs and serve on top of the basmati, together with a dollop of yogurt and perhaps a few Chapati.

**MAKES 4 SERVINGS**

# Luke's Steak with Sautéed Onion Gravy

*V*EGETARIANS may feel aggrieved when they read this, but we think that there is no real substitute for meat. Be sensible, though, and eat only organic meat bought from a reputable farm or butcher. You'll really notice the difference in flavor.

4 organic beef steaks
sea salt and freshly ground black pepper
3 cloves garlic, crushed
2 tablespoons extra-virgin olive oil
Homemade French Fries (page 50)
4 teaspoons organic butter
2 onions, peeled and sliced into rings
4 cups Veggie Stock (page 77)
green beans (optional)

- First, marinate the steaks. Rub the meat with a pinch of salt, lots of pepper, 1 of the garlic cloves, and 1 tablespoon of olive oil. Leave for half an hour while you prepare the onions, etc.
- Heat a large frying pan over a medium flame and drizzle the pan with the rest of the olive oil. Pop the steaks on to cook. We cook our steaks for about 6 minutes per side, as we like them quite well done, but you may feel more or less is better. Follow your taste buds. If you are making Homemade French Fries, put them on now.
- When the steaks are almost cooked, dab each one with some of the butter and add the onions and remaining garlic clove to the pan. Cook the steaks for another minute and then take off the pan. Put the steaks on a plate and keep warm.
- Continue to cook the onions and garlic until soft and brown, then add the Veggie Stock, some more butter, another pinch of salt, and another few twists of pepper. Put a lid over the pan to prevent all those yummy juices from escaping. Cook for 3–4 more minutes, or until the stock has reduced by roughly half.
- Taste the gravy, adjust the seasoning if necessary. Pour the gravy into a serving dish.
- Serve immediately with the Fries and perhaps some green beans. Enjoy your carnivorous feast!

**MAKES 4 SERVINGS**

# "Hearthy" Beef and Thyme Stew

*W*ALKING past a café one day, we saw the sign: "Hearthy Beef Stew served all day." Who are we to quibble? "Hearthy" sounds even more wholesome than "hearty," and this is surely one of the most fortifying meals—excellent on cold winter nights as comfort food. And don't worry about the amount of garlic; each clove will be mellow and delicious by the time you eat it. There really aren't any accompaniments to "Hearthy" Beef Stew other than hot crusty bread for mopping up the juices.

1 tablespoon extra-virgin olive oil
3 teaspoons organic butter
2 onions, peeled and sliced into rings
1 leek, root cut off and sliced
2 carrots, peeled and cut into sticks
1 large potato, peeled and chopped
¾ pound organic beef, cut into cubes
10 cloves garlic, peeled and whole
6 cups Veggie Stock (page 77)
2 teaspoon dried or 1 tablespoon fresh thyme, chopped
sea salt and freshly ground black pepper
Farls (page 156)

- Heat a large saucepan over a low flame and splash in the olive oil and 2 teaspoons of butter. Sauté the onions and leek for 5–7 minutes. When they're soft and translucent, add the carrots and potato. Cook for another 5 minutes. Now push the mixture to one side of the pan.
- Add the beef and the rest of the butter and cook until the beef has lost its meaty color. Throw in the garlic cloves, mix all the ingredients together, and cook for another 4–5 minutes. Stir gently so all the ingredients are well coated in juices.
- Next, add the stock and thyme and season with pepper and salt. Bring to a boil, turn down heat, and let cook on a low heat for 45–50 minutes, until beautiful, bountiful smells are arising from the pot and you can't wait another minute.
- While your stew is doing its thing, make the Farls. Eat your stew hot with plenty of Farls smothered in butter if allowed. Not very sophisticated, says Luke, but damn fine.

**MAKES 4 SERVINGS**

# Peruvian Steak

*W*HEN Mom and Dad were first married, they spent eighteen months in Peru, regularly traveling from the Altiplano down to the selva, or jungle, and the old rubber towns along the Amazon—Iquitos and Pucallapa—where all the local restaurants served this delicious version of steak and onions. Dished up with generous plates of piping hot patatas fritas, you can transform a small, and maybe not completely stunning, piece of meat into a funky feast in minutes.

2 tablespoons extra-virgin olive oil
6 onions, peeled and sliced
3 cloves garlic, peeled and crushed
1 pound good organic steak cut into strips
sea salt and freshly ground black pepper
1 teaspoon organic butter
Homemade French Fries (page 50)
Aioli (page 168)
Harissa (page 171)

- Heat a heavy-bottomed sauté/frying pan over a low to medium heat. Pour in the olive oil followed by the sliced onions (you can't have too many fried onions, so be generous). Sauté the onions until soft, gold, and translucent, about 10 minutes. Then add the garlic and sauté for another minute or two.
- Now move the onion and garlic mixture to one side of the pan. On the other side, pop in your sliced steak pieces. Cook for 8–10 minutes, turning to cook all sides while making sure the onion and garlic mixture doesn't burn.
- When your steak pieces are cooked to your taste, with a wooden spoon or spatula mix all the ingredients together. Season with salt and freshly ground black pepper, top with a teaspoon of butter, and cook for another minute or so, until the butter is completely absorbed.
- Then onto the table with the whole pan (if it's a pretty one!) and allow everyone to help themselves. Serve with a big bowl of Homemade French Fries, a bowl of Aioli and Harissa. Ay Caramba! You'll be beating them back from the table?…

**MAKES 4 SERVINGS**

# Chicken Meals

$\mathcal{N}$ot only do chickens give us chicken soup and the most wonderful white meat, they also give us the universe's greatest packaging feat, eggs. When you are sensitive, chicken is a miracle food packed with protein and taste and yet relatively easy to digest. So much chicken is treated with water and other additives that much of the chicken available is probably actively harmful. So don't forget: always buy free-range, or even better, organic, better for the chickens, better for the environment, and much better for you.

# Brian's Spicy Chicken Curry with Organic Brown Rice

THIS is the perfect medicinal chicken curry! Although this may seem rather bizarre, it's an entirely reasonable suggestion. All the ingredients in chicken curry are in some way supportive to the immune system, which is especially important if you're feeling delicate. This is also a very tasty meal, one of those fabulous recipes that can be cooked on autopilot. This recipe has been designed and perfected by Chupi's boyfriend, Brian, and our many tasting sessions have paid off!

2 tablespoons extra-virgin olive oil
2 onions, finely chopped
2 cloves garlic, peeled and crushed
4 good-sized chicken breasts, sliced into ½-inch strips
1 tablespoon each fresh rosemary and parsley, finely chopped
4 teaspoons each ground cumin and coriander
2 teaspoons turmeric
2–3 teaspoons cayenne pepper or other chili powder
sea salt and freshly ground black pepper
6 cups Veggie Stock (page 77) or Chicken Stock (page 84) or water
2 cups organic short-grain brown rice
4 cups water
Chapati (page 160)
bio-live natural yogurt

- Heat a large saucepan over a medium flame. Heat the olive oil, then add the onions and sauté for 5–6 minutes with the saucepan lid on.
- When the onions are soft, push them to one side and add the garlic and chicken. Cook the chicken until it has lost its pink color, say 5 minutes.
- Then mix everything in the saucepan together and add the herbs and spices. Season generously with pepper and a pinch of salt. Cook for 2–3 minutes more to bring out the flavor of the spices, then add the stock. Bring slowly to a boil, reduce the heat, and simmer gently for 15–20 minutes.
- As soon as the curry is cooking independently, put the rice and water into a saucepan with a tight-fitting lid, and cook for 20 minutes over medium heat.

- While the rice and curry are cooking, make the Chapati, as they'll take a few minutes to prepare and cook.
- The curry sauce will have reduced by half, with gorgeous smells emitting from the pot, when the time to eat has arrived. So serve the curry beside, not on top of, the rice—you will want to be able to taste the plain rice too, with a dollop of yogurt and a Chapati.

**MAKES 4 SERVINGS**

# Bridget Jones Chicken

THIS is the most wonderful—and incredibly simple—dish imaginable. All the ingredients are just roughly chopped, packed into a casserole, drizzled with olive oil, and tossed into the oven. We called it Bridget Jones Chicken because the night we first made it was the night the film came out on video. It was "Chop! Hurl! Grind! Drizzle!" and into the oven you go! And then we all dashed for the sofa and the video.

4 chicken breasts, or thighs, chopped into good-sized chunks
5 potatoes, scrubbed and quartered
a few slices prosciutto or smoky bacon torn into shreds
4 cloves garlic, peeled and whole
2 cloves garlic, peeled and crushed
2 onions, peeled and quartered
1 bulb fennel, chopped into chunks
1 handful fresh rosemary sprigs
juice of half a lemon
3 tablespoons extra-virgin olive oil
sea salt and freshly ground black pepper

- Preheat the oven to 400°F.
- Pack all the ingredients tightly in a good-sized casserole or ovenproof dish, giving everything a good mix to ensure all the ingredients are well coated in oil and herbs.
- Season generously with freshly ground black pepper and sea salt and drizzle with oil.
- Put on the lid or cover with foil and place in the oven. Roast for 1 to 1½ hours, or until the potato chunks are soft through and through.

**MAKES 4 SERVINGS**

# Chicken Provençal

WE love Chicken Provençal—it's one of those dishes that can be eaten at any time of the year and on any occasion whether fancy or simple. It is so easy to make, you just toss everything in to cook and when you can't wait any longer, eat! This dish can be prepared ahead, as the flavor improves wonderfully. It is also delicious in a sandwich.

4 tablespoons extra-virgin olive oil
2 onions, peeled and chopped
12 cloves garlic, peeled and left whole
4 chicken fillets, cut into strips
1 red pepper, deseeded and cut into thin strips
1 yellow pepper, deseeded and cut into thin strips
4 very ripe tomatoes, chopped
3–4 sprigs rosemary
sea salt freshly ground black pepper
1½ cups short grain brown rice

- Put the olive oil into a large pan with a tight-fitting lid and place pan over medium heat.
- Sauté the onions in the olive oil. After 5 minutes, add the rest of the ingredients and cook, stirring frequently, until the chicken has turned white, about 4–5 minutes. Season very generously.
- Put the lid onto the saucepan, and cook for 25–30 minutes, stirring occasionally. While the stew cooks, put the rice on to cook with 3 cups of water over medium heat. Both the stew and rice will be done at the same time.
- Serve together, with a chunk of bread.

**MAKES 4 SERVINGS**

# Roast Chicken with Homemade Gravy

THEY say you can judge a restaurant by its roast chicken. It's definitely one of those things you think you know how to cook, but when you do it, it's hard to get it really scrumptious. Always try to get a really good free-range bird from a reputable farmer or butcher. Here's our simple and tasty version; original and best.

1 good-sized free-range chicken
1 tablespoon extra-virgin olive oil
sea salt and freshly ground black pepper
2 onions, unpeeled
4–5 carrots, scrubbed
3–4 bulbs garlic, unpeeled and whole
several sprigs rosemary, bayleaf, and sage
1 potato, scrubbed
3 slices of bacon
2 teaspoons organic butter (for the gravy)
4 cups Veggie or Chicken Stock (for the gravy) (pages 50 and 84)
Baked Potatoes (page 49)
green beans
Green Salad (page 70)

- Preheat the oven to 450°F.
- Remove any uncookable parts (rubber bands, etc!) from the chicken. Rub the bird all over with the olive oil, season with sea salt and freshly ground black pepper, and place it, breast down, in a large roasting tin.
- Place the onions, carrots, and 1 bulb of garlic around the bird and strew half of the fresh herbs over the bird and veggies. Jam the scrubbed potato into the larger of the chicken's cavities, season again with salt and pepper, and pop into the oven.
- After about 30–35 minutes, remove the chicken from the oven and carefully turn over so the breast is now facing up. Cover the breast with the bacon, making sure the vegetables are all cooking evenly and pop everything back into the oven.
- Cook for another 40–45 minutes. To check if the chicken is properly cooked through, slide a skewer or a slim knife into the thigh meat, slide out, and then press down with the flat of your knife against the incision; if the juices run clear and yellow, it's cooked, if there's still a taint of pink, pop back into the oven for another 10–15 minutes. Once you're sure the chicken is cooked, lift it carefully out of the roasting pan and onto a

**WHAT TO EAT WHEN YOU CAN'T EAT ANYTHING**

serving plate, along with the bulb of garlic and most of the veggies. Keep 1 onion, a few cloves of garlic, 1 carrot, and the potato for the gravy.

- Let your chicken sit, or "rest"—a warming oven is perfect for this, for 10–15 minutes, allowing the juices and delicious tastes to run back into the meat, while you get to work on the gravy.
- With your roasting pan now on top of the stove on a gentle heat, first remove any scorched herbs, etc., then mash down the onion, garlic, carrot, and potato with the back of a wooden spoon. Put in the rest of the fresh herbs and the butter and cook for several minutes.
- Now add the stock. Taste, adjust seasoning, and allow to cook for another few minutes—you're aiming to reduce the stock by about a quarter, and the longer you can bear to leave it, the more scrumptious it will be.
- When you're ready, put the chicken on the table with a fragrant and steaming bowl of gravy alongside. Serve with lots of Baked Potatoes, green beans, and a Green Salad.

**MAKES 4–6 SERVINGS**

# Chicken Sandwiches

THESE scrumptious sandwiches are perfect for picnics and fussy families who like fast food. Ideally these should be cooked as a family, or at least as a two-person affair, to cut down on the work involved. As always, if you've found a bread that's acceptable, use it. We love Farls, they take so little effort and they are impossible to beat, both health- and taste-wise. And don't worry about making the Mayonnaise, it's so easy.

## The Chicken
2 tablespoons extra-virgin olive oil
4 scallions, chopped
4 good-sized chicken breasts, sliced into ½-inch strips
2 cloves garlic, peeled and crushed
1 tablespoon fresh rosemary and parsley, chopped
sea salt and freshly ground black pepper

## The Farls
3 cups white spelt or organic wheat flour
1 teaspoon wheat-free baking powder
¾ cup water or rice, oat, soy, or cow's milk

## The Mayonnaise
2 yolks of free-range eggs
½ cup extra-virgin olive oil
¼ cup sunflower oil
a good squeeze fresh lemon juice
sea salt and freshly ground black pepper

4 handfuls salad leaves/lettuce or
Green Salad (page 70)

- Put the first five prepared chicken ingredients into a large frying pan over medium heat and season well with salt and pepper. The chicken will take about 12 minutes, with occasional stirring to prevent sticking, but if you keep an eye on it, you can let it do its own thing while you prepare the Farls and Mayo.
- The Farls recipe is on page 156, but here are the elements of it. Combine the flour and baking powder. Add the liquid and mix until

**WHAT TO EAT WHEN YOU CAN'T EAT ANYTHING**

you have a soft dough. Split the dough into 4 balls and flatten each into a round ½ an inch thick. Put another pan over medium heat and sprinkle with flour. When the flour starts to brown, place a Farl onto the pan and cook for 3–4 minutes until lightly browned. Flip over and cook on the other side for another 3–4 minutes. Do the others the same way and keep in a warm place.

- Now for the Mayo: combine the two oils, then get a small bowl and put the egg yolks into it. Start by adding the first drop of oil, gently mixing it into the yolks with a small whisk. Add the second drop and mix in again, always making sure to combine the last drop of oil before adding the next. Slowly increase the amount of oil, with care, so that the mixture doesn't curdle. When the egg has absorbed all the oil, add the lemon juice, season with salt and pepper to taste, and set aside.

- The chicken should be just cooked now, so pop it into a serving dish on the table along with the Farls, Mayo, and the Green Salad. Let everyone prepare their own sandwiches at the table—slit open the warm Farls, line with lettuce, pack in the diced chicken pieces, spoon in some Mayo, season generously with sea salt and freshly ground black pepper. Scrumptious!

**MAKES 4 SERVINGS**


## Spiced Chicken Wraps

A spicy, Latin America-inspired variation of Chicken Sandwiches is easy. Add 2 teaspoons each ground cumin, coriander, and chili powder when you're cooking the chicken and use Tortillas (page 154) instead of Farls. Prepare the Wraps by taking the cooked Tortilla, spreading with Mayo, then adding the cooked chicken, then the Green Salad. Lastly, season generously. Roll up and scarf!

# Chili Chicken Dippers

THEY are best served with Fries for the full hit.

2 tablespoons extra-virgin olive oil
1 cup white spelt or organic wheat flour
1 cup water
2 teaspoons ground coriander
2 teaspoons ground chili
2 teaspoons ground cumin
Homemade French Fries (page 50)
3 good-sized chicken breasts, sliced into ½-inch strips
white of 1 free-range egg
a saucepan full of good quality sunflower oil
sea salt and freshly ground black pepper

- Warm the oil over medium-high heat while you prepare the ingredients.
- Sieve the flour into a bowl, make a well in the center, add the olive oil and water and whisk to prevent lumps. Chuck in the spices, mix again, and set the batter aside.
- Prepare the French Fries and pop in to cook as soon as the oil is ready. Cook for about 10 minutes or until golden brown. Meanwhile, prepare the chicken.
- Now back to the batter: whip the egg white until it forms stiff white peaks, then fold the whipped egg white into the batter. Pop the strips of chicken into the bowl of batter. The French Fries should be cooked by now, so put them on a plate covered with paper towels and keep warm while you cook the Dippers.
- Individually pop each dipper into your waiting deep-fat fryer. Cook for roughly 10–15 minutes or until golden brown.
- Serve the Dippers and Fries with Mayonnaise, Zingy Tomato Salsa (page 170), natural yogurt, or any other dips you like, and season well.

**MAKES 4 SERVINGS**

# Yummy Treats

$\mathcal{I}$f you read a "normal" cookbook, you will be forgiven for thinking there is no such thing as a junk-free dessert; if you read most alternative cookbooks, you will be forgiven for thinking that desserts are made only from dried fruit. Gorgeous desserts can be made for sensitive eaters; we've tried to cover every sugar craving, from the cold, sweet, and sparkly Original Lemonade (pg. 140) to the crisp, sophisticated Twice-Baked Biscotti (pg. 137). We hope these inspire you. Remember that these are Green, healthy, nutritious desserts—second or third helpings are not only allowed, but absolutely essential.

# Creamy Ice Lollipops

THIS is a very simple recipe, but it does embody our philosophy: good food does not need to be complicated and Green food does not need to be bland. We can't stress the wonders of ice lollipops too strongly, so just try it.

**2 bananas, peeled and halved widthways**
**3–4 teaspoons local organic honey**

- Push a lollipop stick into each half of the bananas. The honey is optional, but if you are using it, just roll each banana half in the honey.
- Now wrap each half individually in parchment paper.
- Pop into the freezer for 3–4 hours. Scarf straight from the freezer.

**MAKES 4**

# Twice-Baked Biscotti

*W*HOLEFOOD diets are not normally measured in the number of biscuits you can eat, but these are an absolute gem. An Italian recipe, the Biscotti are twice-baked for extra crunch. We've modified them for a more Green diet.

**1¼ cups white spelt or organic wheat flour**
**1½ teaspoons wheat-free baking soda**
**1 cup whole almonds**
**2 free-range eggs**
**3 tablespoons local honey**
**1 teaspoon vanilla extract**

- Preheat the oven to 350°F.
- Mix the dry ingredients in a bowl, make a well in the center, and add the rest of the ingredients. Using your hands, mix everything together until you have a soft, pliable dough, dusting your hands with flour if they get too sticky.
- Lightly oil a baking pan. Shape the dough into a log about 12 inches long and 2–3 inches wide. Flatten the top of the dough with a rolling pin until it's roughly 1 inch thick, then dust with flour. Using a wet knife, score the top of the dough at ½-inch intervals, cutting two thirds of the way down. Bake in the oven for 12 minutes, until pale gold and firm to the touch.
- Remove from the oven and cut fully through the markings. Arrange the pieces cut side down on the tray and pop back into the oven for another 5 minutes.
- Remove from the oven and leave on a wire rack to cool—for as long as you can bear to wait.

**MAKES APPROXIMATELY 25 COOKIES**

> **Hint:** The best thing to eat with Biscotti is carob spread, which is available in most good health food stores. This is a wonderful chocolaty spread that is in fact made from hazelnuts—a total treat when you're off sugar and cream and additive-laden "straight" chocolate. One of the ways of staying off junk food is to eat things like carob—if you're too hard on yourself you won't last, and you'll start incorporating the junk back into your diet. So, be nice to yourself and buy yummy things; in the long term they're not expensive because unlike so much "straight" food, they're not going to make you ill.

# Raspberry and Yogurt Fool

*A* SIMPLE and excellent combination, this gorgeous recipe can be pulled together in minutes, illustrating how a good, Green, healthy dessert does not necessarily mean carrot cake. This is also very easy to digest and good for you. You can use other berries in season, for example blackberries.

1 cup fresh raspberries
2 tablespoons local organic honey
8 ounces of bio-live natural yogurt

- Put the raspberries and honey into a bowl and mash gently, but be careful not to turn them into a total purée.
- Add the yogurt and swirl through the raspberries so that you have pink, streaky fool.
- Serve chilled, or at once if you can't wait, with Shortbread (page 145) if you have time to make it.

**MAKES 2 SERVINGS**

WHAT TO EAT WHEN YOU CAN'T EAT ANYTHING

# Baked Nectarines

THIS recipe was written in the middle of the snow, in minus-degree temperatures in winter. . . . Not very seasonal. However, Baked Nectarines are in fact great in the middle of winter—hot, sweet, and tasty with a gooey raspberry sauce. Stylish enough for the food-for-friends thing, try serving them with natural yogurt and Shortbread—and you really can say "here's something I made earlier."

**6 nectarines, halved and pitted**
**6 tablespoons local organic honey**
**1 cup raspberries**

- Preheat the oven to 400°F.
- Place the nectarines cut side up on a baking tray. Drizzle each with half a tablespoon of honey.
- Divide the raspberries evenly among each half and place in the center. Bake in the oven for 10 minutes.
- Serve 3 nectarine halves per person with the gooey honey, dissolving raspberries, and some Shortbread (page 145).

**MAKES 4 SERVINGS**

# Original Lemonade

THIS makes very tasty lemonade, which is good if you care at all about your body. "Normal" lemonade is pure sugar and junk. We've given a guide amount of honey, so if you like it sweeter just add more. It's always best to use organic lemons, or at least unwaxed ones when you're using the rind, as "normal" lemons are covered in wax! Not very tasty. You can buy unwaxed/organic lemons at most big supermarkets.

**6 cups water**
**4 organic (unwaxed if organic not available) lemons**
**8 tablespoons local organic honey**
**seltzer water**

- Boil the water in a saucepan. Using the thickest setting on your grater, grate the rind down to the pith of each lemon. Add the rind to the pot. Simmer gently for 5–6 minutes.
- While that's cooking, cut the lemons in half and juice them. Now add the honey to the pot. Stir until melted and strain the mixture into a pretty jar. Discard the rind. Add the lemon juice to the jar. Taste to check that it's sweet enough and stir. You now have a lemonade base.
- To serve, fill a glass one third to a half full with the base and top with seltzer and ice.

**MAKES 4 CUPS OF LEMONADE STOCK**

WHAT TO EAT WHEN YOU CAN'T EAT ANYTHING

# Mango Sorbet

$\mathcal{I}$CE cream for kids, sorbet for adults, and heaven for those on a diet of any description.

**1 large very ripe mango**
**2 bananas**
**½ cup rice, oat, or cow's milk**
**local organic honey (optional)**

- Using a sharp knife, take half the skin off the mango and then chop off the flesh, leaving the pit exposed. Peel off the rest of the skin and chop up the remaining flesh.
- Peel both bananas. Slice them up and put the mango and banana into a freezer-proof container. Pop in the freezer for 4–5 hours or overnight.
- Remove from the freezer and put the fruit into a blender. Slowly add the milk. Taste and add honey if it's not sweet enough for you.
- Put back into the container and return to the freezer for another half an hour. Remove from the freezer and serve in 4 pretty bowls.

**MAKES 4 SERVINGS**

# Jammy Doughnuts

THESE doughnuts are inspired by Darina Allen's Balloon Recipe (from *Simply Delicious Meals in Minutes*); we've just made them more accessible. Thanks, Darina. (About the jam: homemade—in your home—is best, but sugar- and junk-free jam will work too.)

sunflower oil for deep frying
1 cup white spelt or organic wheat flour
1 teaspoon wheat-free baking powder
2 tablespoons local organic honey
½ cup rice, oat, or goat's milk
5 tablespoons raspberry jam

- Heat the oil over a medium-high flame.
- Mix the flour and baking powder in a bowl. Make a well in the center and add the honey and milk. Beat to a gloopy consistency. The oil should have been heating up for about 7 minutes now, so get a table-spoon of mixture and, using your finger, push the mixture off the end of the spoon into the hot oil, being very careful. Repeat.
- Cook the doughnuts for 4–5 minutes or until golden. Remove from the oil and drain on paper towels. Cut each doughnut along its middle and put in 2 teaspoons jam per doughnut.
- Serve immediately while still warm.

**MAKES APPROXIMATELY 10 DOUGHNUTS**

WHAT TO EAT WHEN YOU CAN'T EAT ANYTHING

# Honey Flapjacks with Lemon

$\mathcal{F}$LAPJACKS may sound a bit old-school, but they are a wonderful treat when you're really sensitive, as very few people have a problem with honey. They are also similar to "normal" biscuits, so if you're having problems adjusting to a Green diet, they are great. The only problem is not scarfing down the mixture before it gets anywhere near the oven.

4 tablespoons local organic honey
4 tablespoons sunflower oil
1 tablespoon lemon juice, freshly squeezed
2 cups oat flakes
2 cups jumbo oat flakes

- Preheat the oven to 350°F.
- Melt the honey, oil, and lemon juice in a large saucepan over medium heat, letting the mixture come to a boil.
- When melted, remove from the heat. Add the remaining ingredients. Stir and mix until gooey. Spread out on an oiled cookie sheet and pop into the oven for half an hour or until crisp and golden.
- Slice the flapjacks into 1½-x-1½ inch squares while still hot. Allow to cool, then eat at once or store in an airtight tin.

**MAKES 10–12 FLAPJACKS**

# Cheat's Hot Chocolate

*A*'S wrong as this may sound, it really does work. The recipe came to me after I spotted a box of carob powder in our local heath food store and it tastes absolutely perfect. I prefer to use oat milk, but it's a matter of personal choice. As I have said, carob powder can be bought in health food stores but if you prefer, you can use pure, junk-free cocoa powder instead of the carob.

**2 cups oat, rice, soy, goat's, or cow's milk**
**1 heaping teaspoon carob powder**
**1 tablespoon local organic honey**

- Heat your chosen milk over medium heat for 3–4 minutes or until nearly boiling.
- Remove from the heat, whisk in the carob and honey until bubbly. Taste and add more honey if necessary. Serve at once.

**MAKES 2 SERVINGS**

# Banana Brûlé for Brigid, with Sweet Shortbread

BANANA Brûlé is seriously tempting. A highly nutritious dessert, the caramelized honey is to die for and the contrast between the gooey Brûlé and the crunchy, melt-in-your-mouth Shortbread is fabulous. We think Shortbread is essential to Brûlé, so we've entwined the two recipes, but you can of course have just the Brûlé without Shortbread. This is really a children's dessert masquerading as a grown-up's treat.

## Shortbread
1¼ cups white spelt or organic wheat flour
1 teaspoon organic butter
2 tablespoons local organic honey

## Brûlé
5 bananas, peeled and chopped
1½ cups organic bio-live natural yogurt
4 tablespoons local organic honey

- Make the Shortbread first. Preheat the oven to 350°F. Put the flour in a bowl, rub in the butter, add the honey, and mix—you may need to add a drop or two of water to make the dough stick.
- On a floured surface roll out the dough to ½ an inch thickness. Cut into rounds using a normal drinking glass, re-rolling the dough until it is all used up. Pop the Shortbread onto a floured pan and into the oven for 10–15 minutes or until pale gold.
- While the Shortbread is baking, make the Brûlé. Put the bananas, yogurt, and 1–2 tablespoons of the honey into a pretty, flat-bottomed dish. Roughly mash together, smooth down, and put into the fridge to chill.
- Place a heavy-bottomed saucepan over high heat and add the rest of the honey, which will start to bubble. Keep on the heat while stirring for 4–5 minutes until the honey is turning golden, then drizzle over the banana mixture.
- Return to the fridge and leave until the Shortbread is done. Serve together.

**MAKES 2 SERVINGS**

# Live Yogurt with Honey and Almonds

CHUPI first truly appreciated this simple pick-me-up dessert when, having not eaten for thirty-six hours due to the flu, she collapsed at the kitchen table crying "food!" and was revived by three glasses of this wonderful stuff. Hope you enjoy it too. Even if you're dairy intolerant, you may be able to tolerate organic bio-live natural yogurt.

**12 ounces of organic bio-live natural yogurt**
**1 tablespoon local organic honey**
**½ cup whole almonds, halved**

- Get two pretty glasses and divide the yogurt between them. Swirl the honey over each and add the almonds. Serve!

**MAKES 2 SERVINGS**

# Golden Apple with Orange Crumble

THIS is a gorgeous combination of orange crumble and sweet apple. Although Apple Crumble is rather a cliché in wholefood cooking, it's still very tasty, especially during the winter. You need to peel the apples if they're not organic, as there will be a buildup of toxins in the skin. If the apples are organic, you can choose whether to peel them or not.

3 apples, peeled and chopped
½ cup water
juice of 1 orange, freshly squeezed
1 tablespoon organic butter
4 tablespoons sunflower oil
2 tablespoons local organic honey
1 cup jumbo oat flakes
1 cup oat flakes
½ cup wholegrain spelt or organic wheat flour
12 ounces organic bio-live natural yogurt

- Preheat the oven to 350°F.
- Put the apples, water, and half the orange juice into a heavy-bottomed saucepan and leave to simmer over low heat while you prepare the crumble.
- Melt the butter, sunflower oil, and honey in a saucepan. Mix the jumbo oats, oats, and flour together in a bowl. Combine with the honey mixture and the remainder of the orange juice. You have your crumble.
- The apple should be cooked enough by now, so take it off the heat and put it into a lightly greased ovenproof dish. Cover with the crumble and pop into the oven for 40 minutes or until golden brown.
- While the crumble is doing its thing, lightly whip the yogurt using a hand whisk, until it forms soft peaks.
- Serve the crumble with a dollop of the whipped yogurt as an excellent dessert.

**MAKES 4 SERVINGS**

# Carob Brownies or Indulgence Chocolate Cake or Layered Strawberry and Vanilla Cake

*Y*OU want a multipurpose cake recipe that actually works? You got it. We've tried numerous alternative cake recipes with dismal results. The first cake we made didn't even rise, all we got was a flat, dense pancake. However, after much practice, we produced a good, Green cake. The first recipe makes one tray of carob brownies, but the recipe is the basis for two variations. The first is for a vanilla cake layered with strawberries and cream and the other for a chocolate cake layered with chocolate and cream. For the carob powder you can use pure, junk-free cocoa powder if you want.

## Carob Brownies
**4 tablespoons organic butter or suitable unhydrogenated margarine**
**4–5 tablespoons local organic honey**
**2 free-range eggs**
**2 teaspoons wheat-free baking powder**
**3 teaspoons carob powder**
**1¼ cups white spelt or organic wheat flour**
**1 teaspoon vanilla extract**

- Preheat the oven to 350°F. Line an 8-inch square cake pan with parchment paper greased with a little oil or butter. Next, roll up your sleeves!
- Cream the butter and honey together in a bowl until light and fluffy, about 4 minutes—basically you're beating air into the mixture to help it rise. Now lightly beat the eggs together. Sprinkle the baking powder and carob over the creamed mixture, then fold in the flour one tablespoon at a time, alternating with a small splash of eggs (going gently, as you don't want to beat out any of that good air). Keep adding the flour and eggs until you're finished.
- Pour the mix into the prepared pan, smooth down, and pop into the preheated oven for 20–25 minutes.
- Check on the brownies after about 20 minutes. Take them out when they are very nearly fully done, as you want them to retain some moisture. Allow to cool, then cut into squares. If you want to impress, top them with a dollop of yogurt, some carob spread, and a drizzle of honey.

**MAKES 12 BROWNIES**

## Indulgence Chocolate Cake

**Brownie recipe, doubled**
**6 tablespoons organic bio-live natural yogurt**
**6 tablespoons carob spread**
**2 tablespoons local organic honey**

- The great thing about the Brownies recipe is that it's so versatile and can be used to make divine cakes. The quantities above will produce a cake 8 x 1½ inches high, a lovely cake but not really enough if you want to celebrate! Simply double the quantities given above and bake the mixture in two 8-inch round cake pans. (You'll need to bake the cakes for 25–30 minutes, 5 minutes more than for the Brownies.)
- Once the cakes have been baked and cooled, slice each in half horizontally so you end up with 4 layers. Spread the base with 2 tablespoons yogurt, then 2 tablespoons carob spread, then a drizzle of honey.
- Put the next layer of cake on, then another 2 tablespoons yogurt, 2 tablespoons carob spread, and a drizzle of honey.
- Add the next layer of cake, then a final layer of yogurt, a final layer of carob spread, and a drizzle of honey. Finally top with the last layer of cake. If you want to go completely over the top, simply cover the whole outside of the cake with the carob spread. Perfect for birthdays, parties, or indulgence.

## Layered Strawberry and Vanilla Cake

**Brownie recipe, doubled**
**6 tablespoons organic bio-live natural yogurt**
**1 medium-sized container of strawberries, finely sliced**
**2 tablespoons local organic honey**

- If the Indulgence Chocolate Cake seems a bit too chocolaty for you, then there is an alternative. As for the Chocolate Cake, use the recipe for the Brownies and double the quantities. Leave out both the carob powder and carob bar, however, as you want this cake to be chocolate free. Prepare the cake as above.
- Once the cakes have been baked and cooled, slice each in half horizontally so you end up with four layers.
- Spread the base with 2 tablespoons yogurt, one third of the sliced strawberries, and a drizzle of honey.
- Layer with the next slice of cake, then repeat the yogurt, strawberries, and honey combination. Add another layer of cake, then repeat the yogurt, strawberries, and honey combination and top with the last layer of cake. A very impressive summer, birthday, or party cake.

# "Sort of" Danish Pastries

ONCE while in Bath, England, on vacation, we developed a ritual of getting up before everyone else, running to the local bakery, nabbing the first freshly baked sweet Danish pastries, and going to sit by the river to have a pre-breakfast munch. These, a very recent invention, are a Green version and imitate the real ones well, with their sticky-sweet insides.

1¼ cups dates, pitted and chopped
1 cup water
2 cups white spelt or organic wheat flour
2 teaspoons wheat-free baking powder
1 tablespoon organic butter or unhydrogenated margarine
3 tablespoons local organic honey
1 free-range egg
⅕ cup organic cow's, sheep's, oat, or soy milk
white of 1 free-range egg

- Preheat the oven to 450°F.
- First, simmer the dates in a small saucepan over medium heat with the water. Leave for about 7 minutes while you prepare the pastry.
- Combine the flour and baking powder in a bowl. Rub in the butter. Make a well in the center and pour in the honey, egg, and milk. Mix with a blunt knife until the pastry comes together, then roll out on a floured surface to about ½-inch deep x 12 x 18 inches.
- The dates should be in a suitable goo by now. If not, mash with a fork until smooth. Spread the date mixture evenly over the rolled-out pastry. Now roll up the dough as if it were a Swiss roll, along the longest side, tucking the pastry in as tightly as you can without tearing it. You should have an odd-looking log, which you then slice up into 14 pieces, or whirls, about every 1 inch.
- Dust your hands and a large baking sheet with flour and gently flatten each whirl out about 1 inch thick. Lay them on your floured baking pan and, using a pastry brush, brush each pastry with some egg white.
- Put into the oven for about 12–15 minutes. Remove and allow to cool before scarfing.

**MAKES APPROXIMATELY 14**

# Excellent Breads

$\mathcal{O}$f all intolerances, in our opinion, wheat and yeast really are the worst. When you can't eat bread you feel so light—whoever said bread was the staff of life wasn't joking. If you have to give up ordinary wheat—what's available everywhere—finding a good substitute that actually replicates wheat can be a nightmare. We eventually found spelt—flour grown at high altitudes and dating from Roman times, that hasn't been mauled with pesticides, etc. It's the most wonderful food and even really sensitive people can tolerate it.

By far our best bread find, however, has been Farls, the most wonderful buns/rolls/naans you could get—that is without including a yeast colony or two. If you haven't been eating bread, they are the first thing you should try. We have also included two gluten-free breads for super-sensitive people, even though we find spelt acceptable. As the French—master bakers of the universe—would say, *"Un jour sans pain c'est un jour sans soleil."*

# Yummy Soda Bread

*W*HEN you can't eat yeast, it seems impossible to find a decent bread; this gap, however, is happily filled by traditional Irish Soda Bread. If you don't have enough time to make your own, some of the store-bought soda breads are OK if you're not wheat intolerant; otherwise, try this tasty recipe.

**3 cups wholegrain spelt or organic wheat flour**
**1 cup white spelt or organic wheat flour**
**1 teaspoon wheat-free baking powder**
**1 cup rice, oat, soy or buttermilk**
**1 tablespoon bio-live natural yogurt**

- Preheat the oven to 450°F.
- Put the flours and baking powder into a mixing bowl and combine. Make a well in the center, slowly add whichever liquid you've picked and the yogurt, mixing with a wooden spoon. You should have a soft, not too sticky dough.
- Gently form the dough into a round ball, place on a floured baking pan, and cut 1-inch-deep parallel cuts about 1 inch apart.
- Pop into the oven for 35–40 minutes or until the bread sounds hollow when tapped.
- When done, remove from the oven, turn upside down on a rack, and allow to cool before serving.

**MAKES 1 MEDIUM LOAF**

## Olive Bread

**ingredients for Yummy Soda Bread**
**3 tablespoons extra-virgin olive oil**
**½ cup black kalamati olives, pitted and finely chopped**
**½ tablespoon fresh rosemary, finely chopped**

- A savory version of Yummy Soda Bread, this is really good when you feel like something a little more sophisticated. It's especially good with cheese. Simply add the oil, olives, and rosemary to the mix and proceed as above.

## Tomato and Fennel Bread

**ingredients for Yummy Soda Bread**
**3 tablespoons tomato passata**
**2 tablespoons extra-virgin olive oil**
**½ tablespoon fennel seeds**

- Another version of Yummy Soda Bread, sweet with a hint of aniseed. Add the tomato passata, olive oil, and fennel seeds to the mix and proceed as above.

# Doña Theresa's Corn Tortillas

DIVINE Latin American food! Corn tortillas are fabulous if you're eating Green, because they're suitable for everyone, including celiac sufferers. Just fill with whatever you feel like, roll up, and enjoy. They're also wonderful as an accompaniment to spicy dishes to scoop up excess juices. When we need Corn Tortillas, we tend to take the easy route and go straight to the experts. So we asked the people behind Sabores de Mexico, the Mexican food people, to create our Tortilla recipe so you can experience Mexico in your kitchen. Now, over to Doña Theresa.

**3 cups corn flour**
**½ teaspoon sea salt**
**1½ cups tepid water**

- Corn Tortillas are widely used in central and southern Mexico and have formed a pivotal part of the Mexican diet since the earliest Mixteca and Mayan peoples. Be sure to buy corn flour (verify it's GE free), sometimes called *masa harina*. Avoid using polenta or cornmeal for tortillas.
- Mix the flour, salt, and water to form a ball of dough. Knead the dough until smooth, about 10 minutes. Cover it with a cloth and leave to sit for 1 hour. The dough will be brittle, so be careful.
- To make the tortillas, take a small amount of the dough and form it into a little ball in your hand. Place the ball between two pieces of plastic (use a plastic food bag cut in half, or any other suitably heavy plastic). On a floured surface, roll it out until it measures 2¼ inches (you can't make them any bigger, or they will disintegrate) and is quite thin, about ⅛ of an inch. With practice you can make them even thinner.
- Put a dry, heavy-bottomed pan on high heat. Once the pan is hot, take the Tortilla in your hand and peel off one side of the plastic. Lightly flip the Tortilla onto the hot pan, peel off the other side of the plastic, and allow the Tortilla to cook for 30 seconds on each side or until it blisters a little. Remove to a clean dish towel and cover as you continue with the rest.
- Keep in a warm place until you are ready to eat. Tortillas freeze well, so any you don't eat can be stored for later.

**MAKES APPROXIMATELY 24**

**WHAT TO EAT WHEN YOU CAN'T EAT ANYTHING**

# Flour Tortillas

As you may have noticed, Corn Tortillas tend to be pretty small. If you want big ones, you have to replace the corn flour with 1 cup wholegrain and 2 cups white spelt flour. If you want very light tortillas, use 3 cups white spelt flour. Continue as above, but make the Tortilla 8 or 9 inches wide and the same thickness as above. To cook, follow instructions above. Of course, these Tortillas are not gluten free.

# Farls

$O$NE of the biggest problems with not being able to eat yeast is the lack of chewy bread or rolls to enjoy. There only ever seem to be rock-hard sourdoughs or bitter, wafer-thin rye crackers, neither of which is much use in sandwich making. These Farls, on the other hand, are gorgeous—even Luke, who is addicted to French bread, will happily munch a Farl. You'll never have to bemoan your breadless state again. Below we've included a few variations on our basic Farl recipe and hopefully these will inspire you to experiment.

**3 cups white spelt or wholegrain spelt or organic wheat flour**
**1 teaspoon wheat-free baking powder**
**¾ cup water or rice, oat, soy, or cow's milk**
**1 tablespoon bio-live natural yogurt**

- Put the flour and baking powder into a mixing bowl and combine. Pour in your chosen liquid and the yogurt, mixing with a knife (strange, I know, but it works), until you have a soft, dry dough.
- You can shape the Farls as you please, but the traditional way is to form the dough into a ball and roll out into a circle less than ¼-inch thick and slice into 4 quarters.
- Put a heavy-bottomed pan on medium heat and sprinkle with flour. When the flour starts to brown, place a Farl onto the pan and cook for 5–6 minutes per side until lightly browned.
- Take the Farl off, sprinkle some more flour onto the pan, and continue with the rest.
- Keep in a warm place until you're ready to eat.

**MAKES 4**

## Olive Bread Farls

### Ingredients for Farls
3 tablespoons extra-virgin olive oil
¼ cup black kalamata olives, pitted and finely chopped
½ tablespoon fresh rosemary, finely chopped

- A savory version of Farls, these are really good when you feel like something different and are especially good with cheese. Simply add the olive oil, olives, and rosemary to the above. Mix and cook as above.

## Naan Bread Farls

### Ingredients for Farls
3 tablespoons extra-virgin olive oil
¼ cup black kalamata olives, pitted and finely chopped
½ tablespoon fresh rosemary, finely chopped

- To be honest, these aren't any different from normal Farls, they are just shaped differently! But I so adore Naans—and my version of them—that I had to include this. When you have the ball of dough, divide it into 4 pieces. Roll each piece into an oval that's slightly bigger at one end than the other.
- Cook as above and serve with Indian foods in place of real Naan breads.

# Cheese and Chive Scones

THE cheese and chives provide contrast and add a yummy taste to the scones. They can be whipped together in a few moments and served with a bowl of soup as a nutritious, tasty meal or eaten as a snack at any time.

2 cups wholegrain spelt or organic wheat flour
1 teaspoon wheat-free baking powder
1 tablespoon fresh chives, chopped
1 lump organic sheep's, goat's, or cow's cheese
¾ cup water or buttermilk
1 tablespoon bio-live natural yogurt (optional)

- Preheat the oven to 450°F.
- Combine the flour and baking powder. Add the chives and cheese, then the water or buttermilk, and yogurt if using. Mix well. You should have a soft, not too sticky dough.
- Divide in half, then each half into thirds, so that you have 6 round balls of dough. Place on a baking pan dusted with flour and pop into the oven for 15–20 minutes or until the scones sound hollow when tapped.
- Allow to cool, and serve as a savory accompaniment to soup or as a snack.

**MAKES 6 SCONES**

## "Unwholefood" Cheese and Chive Scones

- Cheese and Chive Scones are very wholesome and would pass muster in any vegan restaurant. However, sometimes one feels like a scone that's a little lighter. For "unwholefood" scones, replace the wholegrain spelt or organic wheat flour with an equal weight of white spelt or organic wheat flour, add another lump of cheese, and the yogurt.
- Bake as above.

# Five Star Toasted Seed Scones

**Ingredients for Cheese and Chive Scones (minus the cheese and chives)**
1 tablespoon poppy seeds
1 tablespoon sesame seeds
1 tablespoon sunflower seeds

- If your craving something a little different, how about seed scones? Prepare the scones as above up until just before you pop the scones into the oven, leaving out the cheese and chives.
- Take 2 of the uncooked scones and roll in the poppy seeds, 2 in the sesame seeds, and the remaining 2 in the sunflower seeds. Dust a baking pan with flour, put one of the scones in the center, and arrange the others around it.
- Bake as above.

# Chapati

THESE are so fabulously good. Chapati are a very flat bread, like a tortilla but Indian in origin and perfect for scooping up the juices of any spicy meal. We serve Chapati with all Indian foods.

**2 cups white spelt or wholegrain spelt or organic wheat flour**
**⅘ cup water**

- Mix the ingredients together to form a softish dough. If you have the time, let it rise for half an hour.
- Break the dough into 8 equal pieces. Roll each piece into a ball, then flatten into a circle roughly 6 inches wide and paper thin. You may need to use more flour, as this tends to make very sticky pastry.
- Heat a frying pan over a medium flame and dust with flour. When the flour starts to brown, pop a circle on the pan and cook for 3 minutes per side or until it's puffed up. Repeat with the remaining circles.
- Keep warm until you are ready to eat. Serve with Indian foods or use as a wrap for making sandwiches.

**MAKES 8**

# A Green Brown Bread

THIS was our first loaf of cuttable, toastable bread, a major feat. It's not the very Greenest of breads, as we use buttermilk, although as buttermilk contains lots of good bacteria, it isn't that bad. It's so tasty, and normal, that I'm sure you'll forgive us.

1 cup white spelt flour
1 cup wholegrain spelt flour
1 tablespoon wheat-free baking powder
⅓ cup pinhead oats
⅓ cup oats
⅓ cup spelt germ or oat germ
1 cup buttermilk or oat milk and bio-live natural yogurt mixed
1 free-range egg
1 tablespoon local organic honey
1 tablespoon sunflower oil

- Preheat the oven to 400°F.
- Put the two flours and baking powder in a large bowl and mix well to distribute the baking powder. Now add the pinhead oats, oats, and germ. Stir again, make a well in the center, and pour in the milk, egg, and honey. Combine the mixture. It will be very wet and sticky, so stir really well to get the bits left at the bottom of the bowl. Let the dough stand for 5 minutes to allow the baking powder to start bubbling.
- In the meantime, oil a standard bread pan with sunflower oil. Now pour (I did say it was going to be wet!) the dough into your greased pan and pop into the preheated oven. The bread will take about 45 minutes, but check after 40 minutes. The loaf is done when it's golden brown.
- Take out of the oven and allow to stand for a few minutes. To remove the loaf from the pan, hold the top of the loaf, turn upside down, and smack the base of the pan.
- Wrap the loaf in a dish towel and allow to cool before cutting. Store in an airtight container for up to a week, if it lasts that long!

**MAKES 1 MEDIUM LOAF**

# Rosemary Focaccia

*A*S we have said before, when you're on a diet, good breads are hard to find, so this Focaccia, which makes a beautiful olive oil flat bread, is fantastic. Have it on its own or, as we eat it, with savory goodies—"Sun"-dried Tomatoes (page 47), a few really tasty sheep's, goat's, and cow's cheese (for Luke!) and a Green Salad (page 70). Our lazy roast dinner or, as Mom feels it should be, just an appetizer before the real meal!

1½ cups white spelt or organic wheat flour
½ cup wholegrain spelt flour
½ tablespoon each fresh rosemary and thyme leaves, finely chopped
1 teaspoon wheat-free baking powder
1 cup buttermilk or oat milk and bio-yogurt mixed
3 tablespoons extra-virgin olive oil
sea salt and freshly grated black pepper

- Preheat the oven to 400°F.
- Combine the two flours, the herbs, and baking powder in a large bowl, mixing well so that the baking powder is evenly distributed. Make a well in the center of the flour and pour in your chosen liquid and the olive oil. Using a blunt knife, mix until the dough just comes together. Now get your hands into the dough and turn once or twice.
- Oil a cookie sheet. Roll the dough out on a floured surface and then lay it out on the sheet. Drizzle with olive oil, season with salt and pepper, and pop into the oven for 15–20 minutes or until golden brown.
- Take out of the oven and eat immediately while hot. Serve with "Sun"-dried Tomatoes, cheeses, or in chunks with a meal.

**MAKES 1 MEDIUM LOAF**

# Dr. Nancy Dunne's Gluten-Free Bread

DR. Dunne is a lifelong friend of Patricia and Michael Quinn, and a lifelong worker in the field of health. This is her bread for when you can't take gluten in any form.

⅓ cup rice flour
⅓ cup corn flour
4 heaping teaspoons gluten-free baking powder
yolks of 2 free-range eggs
1 cup organic buttermilk or soy milk
2 tablespoons sunflower oil
whites of 2 free-range eggs, beaten till stiff

- Preheat the oven to 375°F.
- Mix the two flours and the baking powder together, stirring well, as gluten-free flours are very fine.
- In another bowl combine the egg yolks, milk, and oil. Slowly pour into the flour mixture, beating to prevent lumps. Fold in egg whites. The consistency should be slightly firmer than pancake batter, but not stiff like cake mix.
- Pour into an oiled pan lined with parchment paper. Bake in the oven for 1 hour. The bread is baked when it turns golden brown. Don't worry if you think the bread hasn't risen—this type of bread doesn't! Gluten-free bread is best served toasted.

**MAKES 1 SMALL LOAF**

# Green Condiments

$\mathcal{I}$f you have any form of allergy, sauces and condiments are an extremely problematic area because they're usually highly processed and full of junk. They should make you go "wow" when they hit you with their amazing natural flavors, but not because they contain sugar, MSG, or tons of salt. The only solution is to make your own at home. All our sauces take only a few minutes to make, ready to be whipped together when called for. Green Condiments are also a great way to get into cooking—it's so hard to get something like Harissa wrong, you'll feel inspired to try the rest of our delicious recipes!

# Classic Tomato Sauce

TOMATO sauce is one of the most versatile sauces in the world. You can use it in so many different ways—with pizza or pasta, with Baked Potatoes (page 49) or Homemade French Fries (page 50). This sauce is a sort of ketchup replacement, but it tastes so much better!

2 onions, peeled and chopped
3 cloves garlic, peeled and crushed
3 scallions, cleaned and chopped
2 tablespoons extra-virgin olive oil
2 pounds of canned tomatoes, chopped
1 cup tomato passata
1 tablespoon fresh basil, torn
few sprigs rosemary, chopped
sea salt and freshly ground black pepper

- Sauté the onions, garlic, and scallions in the olive oil for 8–10 minutes over medium heat with the saucepan lid on. Stir occasionally to prevent sticking.
- When the onions are soft, add the tomatoes, passata, and herbs. Season generously with salt and pepper. Cook for another 15–20 minutes, until the flavors of the sauce have fully developed.
- You can liquidize the sauce or leave it as is, depending on what you want to use it for. Use immediately or allow to cool. Store in the fridge for 3 days or freeze and reheat when required.

**MAKES APPROXIMATELY 2 CUPS**

# Fake Garlic and Herb Butter

*M*OST people like garlic butter, so if you have to remove it from your diet, you can replace it with this recipe. The only real work is peeling the garlic cloves. It's much better for you than "normal" garlic butter, whether you are dairy intolerant or not, and it can be used as a dip, spread, or as a sauce. It will keep for up to a week in the fridge.

3 cloves garlic, peeled and crushed
3 tablespoons extra-virgin olive oil
2 teaspoons organic butter, preferably warm
½ tablespoon flat-leaf parsley, finely chopped
¼ tablespoon rosemary, finely chopped

- Combine all the ingredients in a small bowl, mixing well to ensure the butter and oil blend. These two ingredients are not going to love each other totally, so just give a mix before you use it to ensure you get a bit of everything.
- Serve as a dip, spread, or sauce.

**MAKES 4 SERVINGS**

WHAT TO EAT WHEN YOU CAN'T EAT ANYTHING

# Feta and Sage Relish

THIS sweet/savory relish is good with roast potatoes, on top of toast, or as a sand-wich filling.

1 tablespoon extra-virgin olive oil
1 teaspoon organic butter
2 cloves garlic, peeled and crushed
1 onion, peeled and finely chopped
about 12 fresh sage leaves, finely chopped
2 teaspoons dried or 1 tablespoon fresh basil
1 chunk your favorite cheese (we use feta)

- Warm the olive oil and butter in a heavy-bottomed saucepan. Add the garlic and onion. Sauté for 5–6 minutes until the onion is soft and translucent.
- Add the sage, basil, and cheese a minute before you serve, stirring so that the cheese melts.
- Serve with a roast potato, a fresh Farl, or as a sandwich filling.

**MAKES 4 SERVINGS**

# Mayonnaise

*M*AYONNAISE from a jar is at worst full of horrendous chemicals, emulsifiers, and preservatives, at best loads of sugar vinegar. It takes only a little skill to make up your own—try this and you'll never buy another jar. For health reasons, use the best free-range, or even better, organic eggs. This will keep for several days in a jar in the fridge.

½ cup extra-virgin olive oil
¼ cup sunflower oil
yolk of 1 free-range egg
a good squeeze fresh lemon juice
sea salt and freshly ground black pepper

- There are several secrets to making Mayonnaise: 1. Use a small whisk, about half the size of a normal whisk. 2. Warm the bowl you're using to make the Mayo by filling with boiling water, then emptying and drying thoroughly. 3. Try to have all your ingredients at room temperature. 4. Go slowly when adding the oil. 5. Have confidence!
- Start by combining the two oils, then get a small bowl, warm it, and put the egg yolk into it. Add the first drop of oil, gently mix it into the yolk. Add the second drop, mix in again, always making sure to combine the last drop of oil before adding the next. Slowly increase the amount of oil—if you're not careful, it will curdle.
- When the egg has absorbed all the oil, add the lemon juice and season to taste with salt and pepper. And here's Mom's magic Mayo cure: Don't panic if the Mayonnaise curdles. Take a fresh egg yolk, a new bowl, and slowly add the curdled mixture to the new yolk.
- Use as a dip, sauce, salad dressing, in sandwiches, or whatever you want.

**MAKES 4 SERVINGS**

## Aioli

Aioli is garlic mayonnaise, absolutely delicious and better than ordinary Mayo for that extra zing. Just add 1 clove garlic, peeled and crushed, to the egg before you start adding the oil.

# Yogurt Herb Mayonnaise

This is a creamier Mayonnaise that can be used as normal Mayo, but is better suited to people who like a mild Mayonnaise. Simply add 4 tablespoons organic bio-live natural yogurt, 1 tablespoon fresh chives, parsley, rosemary, or mint or a mix of the four, finely chopped, once the Mayo is made, to either the Mayonnaise or Aioli recipes.

# Zingy Tomato Salsa

WE are addicted to the salsa from Temple Bar Food Market and this is our attempt to re-create its peppery tomato taste. Salsa is an excellent accompaniment: with a toasted Farl, some goat cheese, atop a burger, or as part of a light salad lunch. Try and make the salsa a few hours before you plan to eat it, to allow time for the flavors to develop.

3 scallions, finely chopped
3 cloves garlic, crushed
1 tablespoon extra-virgin olive oil
7 raw very ripe tomatoes, chopped
1 teaspoon each ground cumin, chili powder and coriander
1 tablespoon each fresh parsley and coriander, finely chopped
sea salt and freshly ground black pepper

- Mix the first 6 ingredients together and season generously with salt and pepper. Salsa can be stored in the fridge with a covering layer of olive oil for 3–4 days.
- Serve as a sauce, topping, dip, or sandwich topping.

**MAKES 4 SERVINGS**

## Zingier Tomato Salsa

If you want to further enliven the Salsa, add 1 medium-hot chili, very finely chopped, to the above.

WHAT TO EAT WHEN YOU CAN'T EAT ANYTHING

# Harissa (Chili Relish)

WHEN you're eating Green, suitable sauces are one of the hardest foods to locate. We use Harissa to pep up many different foods, such as burgers (veggie or not) and sandwiches. Just be careful not to add too much. Harissa will keep for days in the fridge, as long as you renew the layer of olive oil.

9 medium-hot red chilis, deseeded and roughly chopped
1 tomato, chopped
4 cloves garlic, peeled and chopped
1 teaspoon each ground cumin and coriander
1 tablespoon flat-leaf parsley, chopped
3 tablespoons extra-virgin olive oil
sea salt and freshly ground black pepper

- Mix the first 6 ingredients to a smoothish consistency in a blender. Season generously with salt and pepper.
- Store in a screw-top jar with a sealing layer of olive oil.

**MAKES 1 JAR**

# Green Basil Pesto

*P*ESTO is so trendy, but also very healthy, as long as you make it at home. The store-bought gunk isn't worth eating. Roasting the pine nuts is optional—they taste better, but if you're very rushed then they are fine unroasted. Pesto is multifunctional, and you can use it in association with breads and pastas for the best results.

**1 cup very fresh pine nuts**
**3 tablespoons extra-virgin olive oil**
**1 squeeze fresh lemon juice**
**1–2 cloves garlic, peeled and crushed**
**4–6 handfuls fresh basil, finely chopped**

- Preheat the oven to 450°F.
- Lay the pine nuts out on a baking sheet and pop into the oven for 10–15 minutes or until the nuts are golden brown.
- If using a pestle and mortar, chop up the basil then crush all the ingredients in your mortar. If using a blender, blend all the ingredients. With a mortar and pestle you will get a rougher, chunkier Pesto.
- Serve as a dip or sandwich filling, with organic pasta or thinly spread across a hot piece of toast. Provided you keep a thin layer of olive oil over the pesto—renewed every time you use it—it will keep for a week or two in the fridge.

**MAKES 1 JAR**

WHAT TO EAT WHEN YOU CAN'T EAT ANYTHING

# Acknowledgments

TO **PATRICIA AND MICHAEL QUINN**, the world's greatest nutritionist and enthusiast respectively. Thank you so, so much.

To Mary, Philip, and Peter, our darling friendies. To Kali, Jay, and Siobhan, glad you like the pizza! To Libby and Naoise, dedicated tasters. To Emma, Matt, Brigid, Holly, and Hazel, we love you guys! To Ruadhri, the adventurous vegetarian. To Eithne, for all the wonderful reviews she is going to give us. To Anna, Catherine, and Libby, for the props. To Barry, fervent thanks for the moral support. To Doña Theresa, *muchas gracias*. To Francie, the kitchen counter king. To Ger Nichol, the queen of literary agents. To Will the Postie, cheers for the fantastic veggies. To Deirdre McQuillan, thank you, thank you, thank you! To the Durneys, for all the garlic and publishing advice. To Yardy, Muttly, and Felix, our underfed garbage cans. And to Brian, Webmaster extraordinaire: check out www.whattoeat.net.

To the publishers of the Irish edition: Eveleen Coyle, who saw promise in our scribbles. To D. Rennison Kunz for guiding our darling book through the final stages. To Michael Gill for his enthusiasm (and for giving us our photos!). To Nicki Howard and Anita Ruane for our cover—although Luke thinks there should be more of him!

—Chupi and Luke Sweetman
www.whattoeat.net

# Index

**INDEX**